GOLDCOIN

HISTORY OF THE FIRST YEAR

A DECENTRALISED CRYPTOCURRENCY
PART OF THE "ALT-ERNATIVE" BOOK SERIES

GoldCoin—History of the First Year

by Christopher P. Thompson

Copyright © 2016 by Christopher P. Thompson

Book Author by Christopher P. Thompson

Book Design by C. Ellis

ISBN—13: 978-1533512833
ISBN—10: 1533512833

GOLDCOIN

HISTORY OF THE FIRST YEAR

A DECENTRALISED CRYPTOCURRENCY
PART OF THE "ALT-ERNATIVE" BOOK SERIES

CHRISTOPHER P. THOMPSON

ABOUT THE AUTHOR

Christopher Paul Thompson is an avid cryptocurrency enthusiast from the United Kingdom. Born in Bradford, UK and academically educated at the University of York (BSc Mathematics). He has been a keen follower of past and current events in the crypto space since March 2013. His first book called Cryptocurrency "The Alt-ernative" A Beginner's Reference is the first book he has ever written.

Other titles currently available:

"Peercoin—History of the First Year"
"Reddcoin—History of the First Year"
"DigiByte—History of the First Year"
"Dogecoin—History of the First Year"

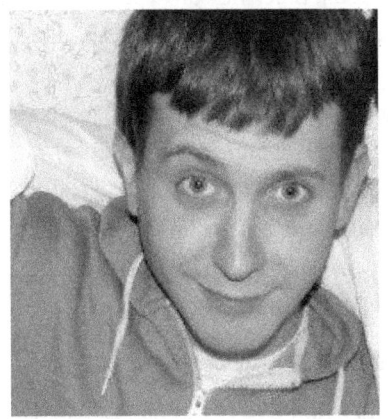

Other titles to be released soon:

"Digitalcoin—History of the First Year"
"Quark—History of the First Year"
"Crypto Bullion—History of the First Year"
"Anoncoin—History of the First Year"
"WorldCoin—History of the First Year"
"Feathercoin—History of the First Year"
"Diamond—History of the First Year"
"Unobtanium—History of the First Year"

E-mail Contact: chris_thompson25@live.co.uk
Twitter Contact: https://twitter.com/MrSilverCider

CONTENTS

CONTENTS

INTRODUCTION

Cryptocurrency was born with the advent of Bitcoin. It was first mentioned in a research paper published online titled "Bitcoin: A Peer-to-Peer Electronic Cash System" with the real name or pseudonym Satoshi Nakamoto attributed to it. This paper was published on the 31st of October 2008. About two months later on the 3rd of January 2009, the Bitcoin network protocol was launched. This technological breakthrough was the beginning of a decentralized public ledger. It allows people to send value across the globe without the permission of a third party authority.

Since then, a growing number of people around the world have been introduced to or discovered cryptocurrency. Many cryptocurrencies have been launched over the following years since the introduction of Bitcoin. The name "alternative" was given to these cryptocurrencies after Bitcoin because they were developed, implemented and introduced to be used instead of or alongside Bitcoin. One could say, a choice of brand in cryptocurrency exists. People have discovered these either through word of mouth, by accident, through personal investigation or via the media. Nevertheless, it has changed the lives of many people. It has provoked the general public into asking innumerable questions about many issues based on subjects such as economics, politics, philosophy, mathematics and so on.

In this book, I hope to give the reader insight into how one particular alternative cryptocurrency began. GoldCoin began in May 2013 as a Scrypt proof of work clone of Litecoin. This book, as well as other future books to be written on other cryptocurrencies, is a historical story of the first year. It covers the time from the initial announcement on Bitcointalk up until the blockchain had been publicly available for one year. In this case, from the 14th of May 2013 to the 15th of May 2014. It also describes the terminology one encounters in cryptocurrency such as proof of work mining, block reward, wallets and so on.

INTRODUCTION

I chose to write about just the first year for various reasons, some of which are:

- For almost all cryptocurrencies, the first year of their existence is the most defining period.

- If I had chosen to write a full history of GoldCoin, I would be continuously playing catch up.

- Most other cryptocurrencies are not several years old yet, so I have limited the scope of all books on individual cryptocurrencies at this time.

- Currently I have a full-time job besides being a cryptocurrency author, so my time is unfortunately limited.

You may have bought this book because GoldCoin is your favourite cryptocurrency. Alternatively, you may be keen to find out how it all began. I have presented the information henceforth without going into too much technical discussion about GoldCoin. If you would like to investigate further, I recommend that you read material currently available online at the official website at www.gldcoin.com.

If you choose to purchase a certain amount of GoldCoin, please do not buy more than you can afford to lose.

Enjoy the book :D

WHAT IS GOLDCOIN?

GoldCoin is a cryptocurrency or digital decentralised currency used via the Internet. It is described as a payment network without the need for a central authority such as a bank or other central clearing house. It allows the end user to store or transfer value anywhere in the world with the use of a personal computer, laptop or smartphone. Cryptography has been implemented and coded into the network allowing the user to send currency through a decentralised (no centre point of failure), open source (anyone can review the code), peer-to-peer network. Cryptography also controls the creation of newly mined GoldCoin units of account.

The GoldCoin network protocol was created by using the source code inherent in the original Scrypt based coin called Litecoin. The developers of GoldCoin altered the code to produce an alternative coin with a differing block reward schedule, block time, difficulty re-targeting algorithm and total number of expected coins.

On the official GoldCoin Bitcointalk thread, GoldCoin is described as:

"Goldcoin is a great name meaning "value" to billions of people Worldwide. Our multi-pool resistant client is innovative and secure with an integrated 51% attack defense system. Goldcoin is a genuinely unique coin, not just another litecoin clone."

As well as the above, the philosophy of GoldCoin as stated by user "MicroGuy" is:

"We need multiple blockchains to mitigate the risks of having a single point of failure. Altcoins provide yet another layer of decentralization. Imagine a world where the only debit card was Discover."

The slogan used by the GoldCoin community to market the coin is:

"THE GOLD STANDARD OF DIGITAL CURRENCY"

WHY USE GOLDCOIN?

Like all cryptocurrencies, people have chosen to adopt GoldCoin as a medium of exchange through personal choice. An innovative feature of the coin, an affinity towards the brand or high confidence of the community could be reasons why they have done so. Key benefits of using GoldCoin are:

- It is a useful medium of exchange via which value can be transferred internationally for a fraction of the cost of other conventional methods.

- GoldCoin eliminates the need for a trusted third party such as a bank, clearing house or other centralised authority (e.g. PayPal). All transactions are solely from one person to another (peer-to-peer).

- GoldCoin has the potential to engage people worldwide who are without a bank account (unbanked).

- GoldCoin is immune from the effects of hyperinflation, unlike the current fiat monetary systems around the world.

IS GOLDCOIN MONEY?

Money is a form of acceptable, convenient and valued medium of payment for goods and services within an economy. It allows two parties to exchange goods or services without the need to barter. This eradicates the potential situation where one party of the two may not want what the other has to offer. The main properties of money are:

- **As a medium of exchange**—money can be used as a means to buy/sell goods/services without the need to barter.

- **A unit of account**—a common measure of value wherever one is in the world.

- **Portable**—easily transferred from one party to another. The medium used can be easily carried.

- **Durable**—all units of the currency can be lost, but not destroyed.

- **Divisible**—each unit can be subdivided into smaller fractions of that unit.

- **Fungible**— each unit of account is the same as every other unit within the medium (1 GLD = 1 GLD)

- **As a store of value**—it sustains its purchasing power (what it can buy) over long periods of time.

GoldCoin easily satisfies the first six characteristics. Taking into account the last characteristic, the value of GoldCoin, like all currencies, comes from people willing to accept it as a medium of exchange for payment of goods or services. As it gets adopted by more individuals or merchants, its intrinsic value will increase accordingly.

GOLDCOIN SPECIFICATION

Since the birth of GoldCoin, its coin specification has changed a few times. At the time of publication of this book, its current specification is:

Unit of account:	GLD
Date of Announcement:	15th of May 2013 at 04:12:12 UTC
Genesis Block Generated:	14th of May 2013 at 19:47:56 UTC
Block Number One Generated:	15th of May 2013 at 00:48:56 UTC
Date of Launch:	15th of May 2013 at 00:48:56 UTC
Founder:	user "gldcoin"
Director/Forum Founder:	Greg Matthews (user "MicroGuy")
Lead Developer:	Amir Eslampanah (user "akumaburn")
Hashing Algorithm:	Scrypt
Timestamping Algorithm:	Proof of Work
Address Begins With:	D or E
Total Coins:	72,245,700 GLD
Block Time:	2 minutes
Difficulty Retarget Time:	60 blocks (120 minutes)
Coins per Block:	4 GLD
Pre-mine:	None

GOLDCOIN MILESTONE TIMELINE

14th of May 2013	—Genesis block timestamped at 19:47:56 UTC
15th of May 2013	—Block number one timestamped at 00:48:56 UTC
15th of May 2013	—Initial GLD Bitcointalk thread created at 04:12:12 UTC
17th of May 2013	—First official forum created at www.gldcointalk.org
19th of May 2013	—First official GLDCoin logo created by "1Peter"
19th of May 2013	—First block explorer created
24th of May 2013	—Cryptsy began active trading of GLDCoin
24th of May 2013	—Original GLDCoin subreddit created at 19:22:30 UTC
28th of May 2013	—Version 0.6.3.2 wallet client released
31st of May 2013	—GLD/BTC trading pair removed from Cryptsy
2nd of June 2013	—First post by user "MicroGuy" on GLD Bitcointalk
5th of June 2013	—Second GLDCoin forum created by "BitcoinBoard"
5th of June 2013	—Third GLDCoin forum created by "MicroGuy"
7th of June 2013	—Mining program to pay miners $8/day began
12th of June 2013	—Website domain www.gldcoin.com acquired for 1 BTC
14th of June 2013	—GLDCoin added to www.coinmarketcap.com
18th of June 2013	—Mining program ended
25th of June 2013	—Official website www.gldcoin.com went live
28th of June 2013	—Facebook group .../groups/gldcoin went live
5th of July 2013	—A future 60 second re-targeting time decided
9th of July 2013	—Lowest market capitalisation of ~$5,143 recorded
19th of July 2013	—A new official coin logo design unveiled
23rd of July 2013	—Version 1.2 wallet client released

GOLDCOIN MILESTONE TIMELINE

2nd of August 2013	—Reward per block reduced from 500 GLD to 45 GLD
6th of August 2013	—https://twitter.com/gldcoin created by user "RichG"
19th of August 2013	—One unit of GLD account surpassed $0.01 (one cent)
21st of August 2013	—CoinEx began to offer active trading of GoldCoin
25th of August 2013	—GLD/BTC and GLD/LTC both on Cryptsy again
31st of August 2013	—Android Wallet released at www.gldcoin.com
3rd of September 2013	—GoldCoin added to http://coinpayments.net
24th of September 2013	—Android Wallet released on the Google Play Store
11th of October 2013	—Version 0.7 wallet client released (mandatory)
21st of October 2013	—Version 0.7.1 wallet client released (mandatory)
24th of October 2013	—Third official Bitcointalk thread created for GoldCoin
31st of October 2013	—At block number 100,000, 51% def algo kicked in
2nd of November 2013	—Version 0.7.1.2 wallet client released (mandatory)
3rd of November 2013	—Version 0.7.1.3 wallet client released (mandatory)
4th of November 2013	—Version 0.7.1.4 wallet client released (mandatory)
10th of November 2013	—Trading on Cryptsy resumed after one week halt.
13th of November 2013	—Version 0.7.1.4 wallet client released (optional)
15th of November 2013	—Android Wallet compatible with 51% Defense Algo
27th of November 2013	—Version 0.7.1.6 wallet client released (mandatory)
27th of November 2013	—Market capitalisation surpassed $1 million
30th of November 2013	—BTC Satoshi value of one GLD went over 10,000
1st of December 2013	—All time high market capitalisation reached
2nd of December 2013	—Version 0.7.1.7 wallet client released
9th of December 2013	—Work began on a future GoldCoin Promotional Video

GOLDCOIN MILESTONE TIMELINE

6th of January 2014	—GoldCoin Promotional Video uploaded to YouTube
10th of January 2014	—www.facebook.com/groups/goldcointalk/ created
18th of January 2014	—GoldCoin "Accepted Here" graphics published
10th of February 2014	—A national political party pledged support for GLD
19th of February 2014	—GoldCoin Foundation website created
24th of February 2014	—A new alternative GoldCoin logo design unveiled
24th of February 2014	—A new GoldCoin slogan unveiled
1st of March 2014	—A song called "Everybody's Doing The GoldCoin Rap" was published
23rd of March 2014	—Third exchange called Bittrex initiated GLD trading
9th of April 2014	—GoldCoin added to the C-Cex voting list of potential coin additions
10th of April 2014	—Update of the wallet client released due to the Heartbleed Bug
16th of April 2014	—Chatbox added to the official GoldCoin Forum
17th of April 2014	—GoldCoin listed on http://bravenewcoin.com
1st of May 2014	—New wallet client almost ready of testing
15th of May 2014	—A total of 169,189 blocks during the first year

PROOF OF WORK (PoW) MINING

Proof of work mining is a competitive computerised process which helps to maintain and secure the blockchain in such a way as to verify transactions and prevent double spending.

In the general sense of cryptocurrency, those who participate in the activity of mining are called miners. They are general members of the cryptocurrency community who dedicate processing power (hash) of their computers towards solving highly complex mathematical problems and verifying transactions. This process upholds the integrity and security of the network. As such, miners are described as protectors of the network. Each transaction (held within a certain block) is validated before adding it to the blockchain. By doing this, they are rewarded (as an incentive) with newly generated mined coins or transaction fees. These coins are issued by the software in a transparent and predictable way outside of the control of its founders and developers. A miner can be based anywhere in the world as long as they have an internet connection, sufficient knowledge of how one mines and the hardware/software required to do so.

Miners use GPUs (Graphical Processing Units) or CPUs (Central Processing Units) to process transactions by hashing. Also, Application Specific Integrated Circuits (ASICs) allow miners to use customised hardware for faster and lower power mining.

Since its launch on the 15th of May, GoldCoin has always had proof of work as timestamping. At the time of publication of this book, miners compete to successfully find blocks which generate four GLD each.

GOLDCOIN BLOCKCHAIN

Every cryptocurrency has a corresponding blockchain within its decentralised network protocol. GoldCoin is no different in this sense. A blockchain is simply described as a general public ledger of all transactions and blocks ever executed since the very first block. In addition, it continuously updates in real time each time a new block is successfully mined. Blocks enter the blockchain in such a manner that each block contains the hash of the previous one. It is therefore utterly resistant to modification along the chain since each block is related to the prior one. Consequently, the problem of doubling-spending is solved.

As a means for the general public to view the blockchain, web developers have created block explorers. The first block explorer for GoldCoin was made available at the domain http://gld.block-chain.net/ thanks to user "503guy". It was announced as being accessible on the 19th of May 2013 on the first official GLDCoin Bitcointalk forum thread.

Since the inception of the first block explorer, other websites have been created. Currently available block explorers include the following:

- http://gld.cryptocoinexplorer.com/;

- https://prohashing.com/explorer/Goldcoin/;

- http://gld.smartchain.cc/;

To be specific, the first block explorer is the officially recognised and trusted website. One can easily access the site by visiting the official GoldCoin website at www.gldcoin.com and then clicking on "Block Explorer" from the "TECHNICAL" drop down menu.

GOLDCOIN BLOCKCHAIN

Block explorers tend to present different layouts, statistics and charts. Some are more extensive in terms of the information given. Some statistics include:

- **Height of block** —the block number of the network.

- **Time of block** —the time at which the block was timestamped to the blockchain.

- **Transactions** —the number of transactions in that particular block.

- **Total Sent** —the total amount of cryptocurrency sent in that particular block.

- **Block Reward** —how many coins were generated in the block (added to the overall coin circulation).

Below is a screenshot of block number one from the block explorer at http://gld.cryptocoinexplorer.com:

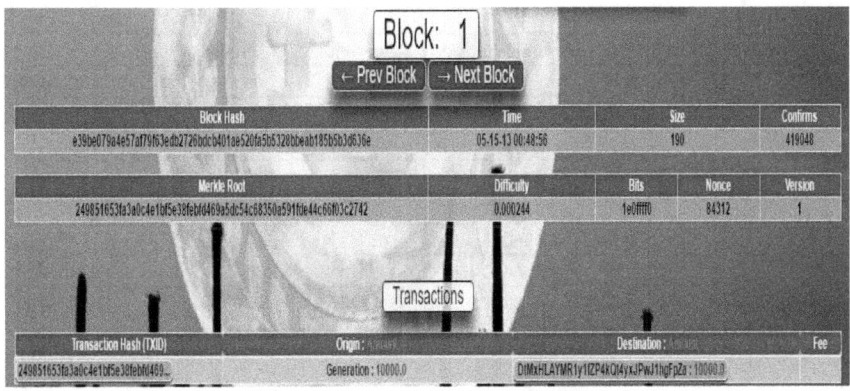

GOLDCOIN BLOCK REWARD TABLE

As time progresses, a certain number of coins (reward) are generated each time a block has been mined, verified and added to the blockchain. As is almost often the case, the reward per block decreases to a lower value at a determined block number.

Initially, the block reward distribution table (see page 38) was set to produce a total of 100 million GLD after 1,170 days (approx. 3.2 years). However, at block number 21,000, either by accident or purposefully, the block reward was set to produce 500 GLD for every block thereafter.

On the 27th of July, version 1.2 of the wallet client implemented a future hard fork at block number 45,000 (see page 64).

On the 31st of October, an innovative fix to the difficulty code became operational.

On the 21st of February 2016, the reward per block reduced significantly to four GLD. As a result, the inflation was drastically cut.

During the first year, a total of about 30,988,050 GLD were mined. Here is the current block distribution table of GoldCoin:

Initial Block	Last Block	Number of Blocks	Reward	Total	Cumulative Total
1	200	200	10,000	2,000,000	2,000,000
201	2,200	2,000	1,000	2,000,000	4,000,000
2,201	21,000	18,800	500	9,400,000	13,400,000
21,001	44,999	23,999	500	11,999,500	25,399,500
45,000	99,999	55,000	45	2,475,000	27,874,500
100,000	169,189	69,190	45	3,113,550	30,988,050
169,190	307,799	138,610	45	6,237,450	37,225,500
307,800	371,999	64,200	31.447	2,018,897.4	39,244,397.4
372,000			4		

BLOCK TIME OF GOLDCOIN

The block time is the average time taken for the network to successfully generate a certain block either by proof of work or proof of stake. Both the reward and time of all blocks generated dictate how the circulation of coins grows over time.

Originally, the block time of the network protocol was pre-determined to permit miners to find one block every 150 seconds (on average). This remained the case after the first hard fork took place on the 12th of June 2013 (17:38:12 UTC). The first twelve blocks timestamped to the blockchain on the 15th of May 2013 were:

Block Number 1	00:48:56 UTC	Block Number 7	01:02:10 UTC
Block Number 2	00:51:59 UTC	Block Number 8	01:04:32 UTC
Block Number 3	00:52:09 UTC	Block Number 9	01:05:39 UTC
Block Number 4	00:52:13 UTC	Block Number 10	01:07:13 UTC
Block Number 5	00:53:04 UTC	Block Number 11	01:10:34 UTC
Block Number 6	00:54:55 UTC	Block Number 12	01:27:27 UTC

As is evident above, it took 2,311 seconds to find the first twelve blocks.

During the last week of the May 2013, transactions were taking a very long time (approx. 3-4 hours) to confirm due to an attack on the network protocol by large miners. The network protocol was in a state of low hashing power (hash) and high difficulty until the next re-adjustment of the difficulty could occur. As a consequence, the community were paid, as an incentive, to add extra hash in order to hasten block generation. Ultimately, the "51% Defense Algorithm" had a significant effect of reducing the chances of attack from large mining operations.

On the 2nd of August 2013, the block time changed from 150 to 120 seconds. It has remained at two minutes until the present day.

GOLDCOIN WALLETS

A wallet is basically a piece of software that can be used on a personal computer, tablet or smartphone. It allows users to store GoldCoin as well as execute transfers of GLD with other users. Alternatively, it can be described as a means to access the coins from the inseparable blockchain (public transaction ledger). The wallet cryptographically generates and holds the public and private keys necessary to make these transactions possible. The software can be accessed, downloaded and installed from the official website by clicking "DOWNLOADS" at:

- http://gldcoin.com

GoldCoin wallets have been developed to work on the operating systems Windows, Mac OS X and Linux. Currently, there are two types of wallet available to the community. These are:

- **PC Wallet Client**: used by those who wish to store their GLD on their own personal computer. Users can generate wallet addresses into which others can send a certain amount of GLD.

- **Android Wallet**: used by those who want to spend their GLD on the go.

On the 14th of February 2016, the latest update of the wallet client was released. Taking effect at block number 372,000, the reward per block reduced from roughly 31 GLD to 4 GLD. Other technical specification changes were:

- Maximum block size Increased from 1MB to 2MB.

- Transaction fee lowered from 0.1 GLD to 0.01 GLD.

- Total generated coins/mining reward fast forwarded twenty years.

GOLDCOIN EXCHANGES

A cryptocurrency exchange is a site on which registered users can buy or sell GoldCoin against BTC, LTC, USD and so on. Some exchanges require users to fully register by submitting certain documentation including proof of identity and address. On the other hand, most exchanges only require users to register with a simple username and password with the use of a currently held e-mail account.

Throughout the first year, the general public were able to trade GoldCoin on three known exchanges. These were Cryptsy, CoinEx ad Bittrex. Unfortunately, the coin no longer trades on these platforms. Both Cryptsy and CoinEx shut down, whereas Bittrex delisted the coin due to lack of trading volume. GoldCoin enjoyed the vast majority of trades on Cryptsy until it closed on the 14th of January 2016.

At the present time, GoldCoin trades on two known cryptocurrency exchanges:

VIEW OF MICROGUY

How did you discover GoldCoin?

"I first encountered GoldCoin while browsing the Bitcointalk.org Alternative Currencies forum."

What attracted you to GoldCoin/cryptocurrency in general?

"Having a business background, I saw GoldCoin as an opportunity to build a currency that could compete with Bitcoin for consumer adoption.

Rarely does the contender with first-mover advantage maintain his or her leading position. Thus, if world history is any indication, it will be a bitcoin competitor that ultimately penetrates the mainstream psyche and wins the race of mass adoption. And the term "Gold" means value to billions of people worldwide, giving us the perfect brand and platform."

How you have contributed to GoldCoin?

"From my perspective, GoldCoin is like a young child, and we the members of this vast community, its vital caregivers. Like a parent, I have tried to provide the basic needs for Goldcoin to succeed. When she falls and scrapes a knee, I apply the band-aid or whichever treatment is needed at the time.

If we all do our jobs properly, one day Goldcoin will mature and walk on her own - resilient, brilliant, and ever-strong."

VIEW OF MICROGUY

Where do you see GoldCoin in the short/long term?

"We intend to make Goldcoin free and decentralized and 100% Blockstream proof. We are building the bitcoin that Satoshi originally envisioned.

And while our competitors focus on micro transactions and payments, our focus is on enhancing the value-storage side of the equation. We have built a practical physical gold replacement that can be used by everyone today as a digital commodity. Our 51% attack defense and Golden River difficulty algorithm give us the strongest most robust blockchain in all of cryptocurrency.

Goldcoin truly is the gold standard of digital currency, a safe haven for value in a turbulent world."

What is your most memorable about of GoldCoin since its launch on the 14th of May 2013?

"This experience has taught me the invaluable lesson in the resolve of the human spirit, the strength of unity, and the unlimited potential of teamwork. When a person is able to see beyond himself and focus attention on serving the greater good of the community - magic happens, mountains move, and Goldcoin and the world change for the better.

When I think back over the past three years, this is the lesson that reflects strongest in my mind."

VIEW OF STOUSE49

"I saw the ANN thread for gldcoin on May 15, 2013, just at about the time when it was first posted. I downloaded the client right away and started mining and was able to mine some of the 10,000 GLD blocks. I stopped mining when the reward was 1,000 GLD and didn't think anything would happen with this coin.

But since I was interested with cryptocurrencies and had bought a ATI graphics card, I was looking at the Alt Coins forum on bitcointalk.org. There were many posts about gldcoin. Many people were excited about it, including one guy with a handle similar to BitshareHashaway. I gave away some of my GLD to various posters on the gldcoin topic. A few weeks later the coin was listed on Cryptsy, so I signed up and started trading as the price dropped. It was about that time I noticed people making fun of **microguy** in the chat box. I think he claimed to have tried to buy some GLD, but the the deal fell through and he might have lost his BTC (not sure though).

Nevertheless, I was somewhat active in the community and joined the first forum that was started called goldcointalk.org. Eventually this forum fell apart and was closed, but gldtalk.org was there to replace it. It was about the same time that there was a 2 GHash/sec mining blitz on the Goldcoin network which pushed the difficulty up. Then the miners left and the difficulty was still high. It took about two or 3 weeks for the difficulty to drop again because the coin was still using litecoins 2016 diff adjustment period.

VIEW OF STOUSE49

The developer of the coin "gldcoin" had offered to help fix that in a fork to change the diff adjustment to 504 blocks with smaller difficulty changes and that helped along with microguy's paid mining to get to the fork. After that I had made some charts that I posted on gldcoin talk for various metrics concerning GLD. One was of the money supply over time and there may have been others. microguy saw these and was interested in my skills and he contacted me and we spoke on the phone. After that I joined the GoldCoin Team along with a few others.

As part of the team, I helped with debugging upgrades on the TestNet and later in the summer I started looking at the source code for the Android wallet for Litecoin and decided to fork it for GoldCoin, even though I had no idea about anything regarding Java or Android. As a programmer, self taught, in C++, I was able to pick up on Java easily and in a few weeks made the GoldCoin Wallet for Android, which I still maintain to this day.

Later that year, the other developer had the idea of a 51% defense, and i helped somewhat with that with the TestNet and code review. After that was implimented, I found that using the block explorer and making charts of difficulty that the difficulty was about to crash to 0 and we were able to fork the wallet to fix that bug. It took a few more fixes to get it working reliably, culminating in the most recent fix called Golden River. Golden River was a fix to the excessively long block times that we were getting based on the previous fixes that were implemented. Sometimes a fix has a side effect. Now the network seems to be running fine.

VIEW OF STOUSE49

I got interested in Bitcoin in March or April of 2013 after hearing about it in the papers, because the price had gone so high. I was fascinated by the computer science behind it all, not so much in the price volatility, though high prices made the mining worth while. I was mining with a card that only could do 400 MH/s, which was good enough to get $10 per week in mining. Of course that was changing as the difficulty for bitcoin increased significantly. But the alt coins were there to keep my interest.

The most memorable moment in GoldCoin history was during the summer of 2013, for our first fork after we had rid our selves of the original developer and the secondary developers that had come to help a little, but were not committed. There was microguy, akumaburn, Sting17 and perhaps a few others. We were counting down for the fork to get the coin back on track with a new mining schedule (which still was at 500 at the time, because the fork to fix the difficulty in the early part of summer had an extra bug of leaving the block reward at 500 forever.) There was the count down, and we were pleased to see that it worked.

Where do I see GoldCoin going? I don't know, but I will be here to keep the Android Wallet working."

VIEW OF AMIR ESLAMPANAH

How did you discover GoldCoin?

I was trading alt-coins regularly on BTC-E and Cryptsy; the latter is how I found it.

What attracted you to GoldCoin/cryptocurrency in general?

Primarily, it was the name itself that attracted me to GoldCoin/GLD. I mean I just didn't think the other coin names were viable for use by the masses. As for crypto-currency in general, a Facebook friend of mine mentioned Bitcoin to me back in Feb of 2013. We're not counting time-travel paradoxes are we?

How you have contributed to GoldCoin?

I have been its lead developer for all but the first month or two.

Where do you see GoldCoin in the short/long term?

Short term we have definitely some marketing challenges to over-come, but I do see us in the top ten crypto-currencies very soon. Long term? Well I can't see the future right? 😐

What is your most memorable about of GoldCoin since its launch on the 15th of May 2013?

That'd have to be the hiring of the "Hobos" on Cryptsy chat.. those were some good times!

VIEW OF GOLDEN_GLITCHER

"Got into goldcoin back in 2013. At the time my life was in tatters, had lost my job, my home and my g/f. Being so depressed all the time i had to get creative in order to pull my mind out of the gutter. Having already been an avid fan of bitcoin from the early days, I was keeping up with everything crypto related . One night at around 4am, in a depressive state, i was watching a tutorial on how to use GIMP, an open source image editing software program. It was in French, to make it even harder. I got frustrated, gave up and started watching crypto related videos. That's when i came across this very excited guy who called himself Micro guy.

The more I watched his videos, the more intrigued I got and less depressed I felt. His enthusiasm was infectious. Even though this guy was making a lot of sense, he just seemed a little bit crazy. I do like crazy so i decided to join his forum. It was a small community at the time but they welcomed me with open arms. Goldcoin then became my life.

I put my head down, got to grips with the image editing software and started making as many promotional images as time would allow for Goldcoin. I wanted other people to be as excited as i was for this crypto currency. I started posting t-shirt designs for fellow members, promotion images for the 100,000 block (which after, goldcoin became '51% attack' safe). Banners ads, fake magazine covers, 'Goldcoin accepted here' logo for people to use on their websites. A bunch of abstract goldcoin images and plenty of images promoting the forum and the official website. It didn't seem like enough though.

I had no job, so with plenty time on my hands i embarked on making the first goldcoin game.

VIEW OF GOLDEN_GLITCHER

It was a side scrolling shoot em up. Micro guy was manning the gold cruiser, making his way through the game, killing various other Alt coin space ships like bbq coin, pandacoin, 42coin and others, you know, getting rid of all the trashcoins. I documented my progress in building the game on the forum and it really seemed to lift everyone's spirits. Unfortunately, I was the only person to play the game. At around 90% completion, my harddrive failed and so too did 6 months of my work. Even though the community were nice about it, I still cringe when I think about it.

All in all, Goldcoin has been a hell of ride with plenty memories. Probably one of the coolest was 'Dec 12th 2013' when Goldcoins marketcap reached over 3.5 million and was worth over 12 cent a coin. Im sure it was around that time Micro guy promised to reenact the naked Miley Cyrus wrecking ball video, on condition goldcoin hit 1 dollar in price. So we all have that to look forward to still.

I have some other memories of an intense rivalry we had with the alt currency called BBQcoin. The coin was useless, it wasn't the least bit inventive, yet it made it into a mainstream media newspaper article. At the time, even bitcoin had trouble getting any attention so they were extremely lucky. What followed were weeks and weeks of Coinmarketcap battles between BBQcoin and Goldcoin. One day, BBQcoin would be just above goldcoin, the next day, Goldcoin would jump back in front. Bear in mind there were only about 30 crypto currencies at that time, competition was fierce.

In the long term, Goldcoin will definitely be a well known and widely used crypto currency. No doubt in my mind. The name is just too universally known and understood to mean a great store of value. Crypto currencies are still a new revolution, once the rest of the world catches up, they'll be wanting some Goldcoin."

GOLDCOIN COMMUNITY

A community is a social unit or network that shares common values and goals. It derives from the Old French word "comuntee". This, in turn, originates from "communitas" in Latin (communis; things held in common). GoldCoin has a community consisting of an innumerable number of individuals who have the coin's well being and future goal at heart. These individuals almost always prefer fictitious names with optional corresponding "avatars". Notable members of the community are "MicroGuy", "akumaburn", "Stouse49", "AZIZ1977" and others.

At the time of publication, there are social media sites on which discussion and development of GoldCoin take place. These are:

- **Facebook**   -https://www.facebook.com/groups/goldcointalk/

- **Official Forum**   -https://www.gldtalk.org/

- **Reddit**   -https://www.reddit.com/r/goldcoin

- **Twitter**   -https://twitter.com/GoldCoin

- **Bitcointalk**   -https://bitcointalk.org/index.php?topic=317568.0

In addition to these, there is an innovative scheme designed to motivate and organise the community's human resources:

- **Open Workforce**   -https://www.gldtalk.org/index.php?topic=3186.0

Workers are assigned a role, report during the week about their work and get paid.

In essence, the community surrounding and participating in the development of GoldCoin is the backbone of the coin. Without a following, the prospects of future adoption and utilisation are starkly limited. GoldCoin belongs to all those who use it, not just to the developers who aid its progress.

FIRST YEAR HISTORY OF GOLDCOIN

LIST OF CHAPTERS

LAUNCH OF THE GLDCOIN BLOCKCHAIN

MAY 2013

I.   Bitcointalk forum thread created for GLDCoin.

II.   The very first coin logo design created and proposed by user "Vikerus".

III.   First official GLDCoin forum went live at www.gldcointalk.org.

IV.   GLDCoin began to trade on the cryptocurrency exchange called Cryptsy.

V.   Version 0.6.3.2 of the wallet client released.

On the 15th of May 2013 at 04:12:12 UTC, a Bitcointalk forum thread was created by a user known by the fictitious forum name "gldcoin". This thread was originally titled "GLDCoin - A Litecoin Based Currency With a More Favorable Block Reward". The first response to this thread was by user "afroman1131" about fourteen minutes later. He said:

> "I shall mine them all with my 2 KH/s lolololo!"

User "scab" replied ten minutes later:

> "...what?"

Block #0 (Reward 0 GLD) May 14th 2013 at 07:47:56 PM UTC

Before the initial GLDCoin Bitcointalk forum thread was created, the genesis block (the first block of the blockchain, but not block number one) had been found, verified and added to the blockchain. It was possible to mine the coin before the initial Bitcointalk forum thread for GLDCoin had been created.

Block #1 (Reward 10,000 GLD) May 15th 2013 at 12:48:56 AM UTC

On the 15th of May, user "Vikerus" proposed the very first coin logo design. At 09:57:15 UTC, the following was posted:

"New Icons for GLDcoins!"

There were claims that the blockchain had split early on, but no-one, including the founder, responded. The difficulty was set low to begin with, so blocks were being mined quickly. Originally, there was a cap of 100 million coins to be generated:

Initial Block	Last Block	Number of Blocks	Reward	Total	Cumulative Total
1	200	200	10,000	2,000,000	2,000,000
201	2,200	2,000	1,000	2,000,000	4,000,000
2,201	26,200	24,000	500	12,000,000	16,000,000
26,201	48,700	22,500	400	9,000,000	25,000,000
48,701	173,700	125,000	200	25,000,000	50,000,000
173,701	673,700	500,000	100	50,000,000	100,000,000

Block #201 (Reward 1,000) May 15th 2013 at 05:37:45 AM UTC

Block #2,200 (Reward 1,000) May 15th 2013 at 10:54:43 AM UTC

Block #2,201 (Reward 500) May 15th 2013 at 10:55:05 AM UTC

On the 15th of May at 19:36:57 UTC, user "faraway" said:

> "I've added a new p2pool.
>
> Here are the parameters:
>
> cgminer --scrypt -o next.afraid.org:8117 -u yourGLDaddress -p .
>
> statistics available here: http://next.afraid.org:8117
>
> 2% fee.
> This one is up, tested, and fully reliable."

This was the first reported mining pool created for GLDCoin. Some users pointed out that they were not receiving pay outs, whereas others said it was working fine. Also on this day, user "Vikerus" created the website domain www.gldcoin.tk and asked the community what could be included there. There were accusations that the coin had been pre-mined, but a few early miners refuted this.

On the 17th of May at 01:13:42 UTC, user "kr4x" said:

> "GLDCoinTalk is UP
>
> http://www.gldcointalk.org/index.php"

On the same day at 01:49:26 UTC, user "vipah" posted that a new mining pool had been set up at http://gld.vircurpool.com (closed on the 21st of November 2013).

Also on the 17th of May, Bitcointalk user "Vikerus" uploaded a video to YouTube titled "How to Mine GLDcoin". By viewing the video, one can see the homepage of the original GLDCoin website (www.gldcoin.tk) as shown immediately below:

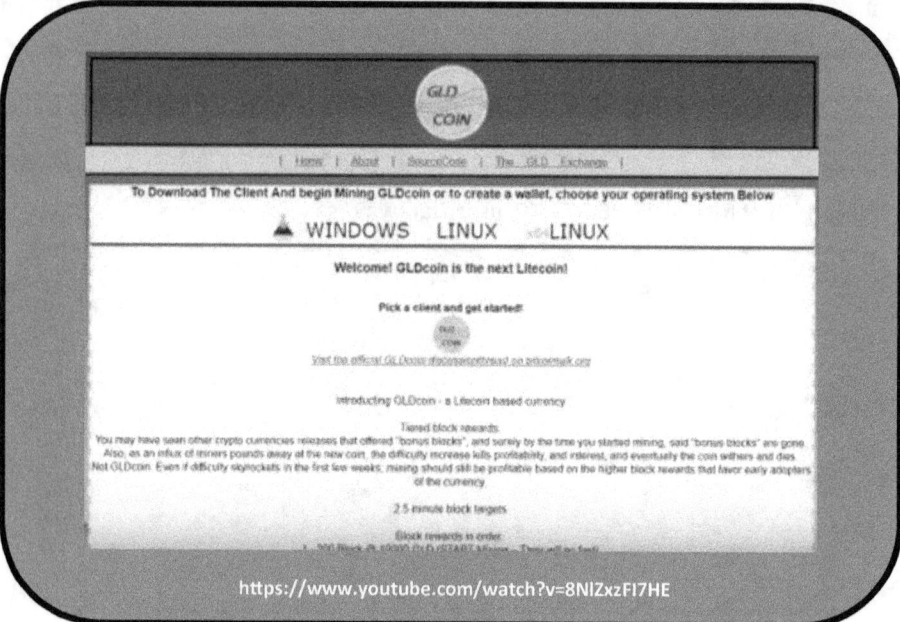

https://www.youtube.com/watch?v=8NlZxzFl7HE

On the 18th of May, two coin logo designs were posted on the official GLDCoin Bitcointalk forum thread by users "BitcoinBoard" (left) and "1Peter" (right):

Three days since the launch of the coin, there were calls for an exchange to add GLDCoin. On a separate designated Bitcointalk forum thread, manual trades were being conducted between those who wanted to buy or sell GLD. A few users had politely e-mailed the Chinese exchange called Bter.com to persuade them to add it.

It had become apparent that user "gldcoin" had been effectively non-existent in terms of contributing to the initial discussion. Some users began to question if the founder had abandoned the coin, or had chosen to stay highly anonymous.

On the 19th of May, a Bitcointalk forum thread was created by user "1Peter" to inform the community of the new official GLDCoin logo:

On the 19th of May at 20:31:05 UTC, user "503guy" informed the community of the first GLDCoin block explorer:

"Block Chain Explorer is up!

Let me know if any issues.

Bounty can be sent to this address: DvMUwdpNQVwSahrBSMuiZDMW6ZW3ybBzQh

http://gld.block-chain.net/"

Users "BitcoinBoard", "kr4x" and "1Peter" were enthusiastic to witness the creation of the first block explorer at http://gld.block-chain.net/. User "BitcoinBoard" created a specific forum thread on Bitcointalk to allow further discussion about it.

On the 20th of May, the first GLDCoin faucet at http://1gld.co.nf/faucet.php was advertised by user "r3wt". He made the source code of the faucet freely available on github later the same day.

On the 21st of May, 16,000 GLD were sold by user "kr4x" to user "majormax" for 8.5 Litecoin (LTC). According to www.bitinfocharts.com, the average value of one Litecoin unit of account on this day was $2.96 . Therefore, the approximate value of one GLD unit of account at this pre-exchange stage was $0.0015725.

On the 22nd of May user "gldcoin" at 19:45:30 UTC posted his opinion about the recent wallet client issues:

> "All, FYI on the wallet trying at times to re-sync. This is someone trying to attack the network through offline mining of the blockchain. They then try to force it onto the network (to get all the coins they mined offline), but the other nodes catch it and ban their IP automatically after a while. They obviously know the other nodes will reject this, but they try anyways because it acts like a denial of service.
>
> Once the network has enough nodes/miners, we won't have this issue, because likely other nodes will ban them before you even see it. This code as far as the wallet goes is identical to litecoin. Only modifications are on the reward/difficulty logic.
>
> You usually only see this on coins with low hashrate. Once we are added to an exchange (within a few days I am told - can't say where), and more people start mining (because it will be worthwhile for for them), these issues should cease."

On the 24th of May, a GLDCoin Skype Support Group on Bitcointalk was initiated by user "BitshireHashaway" who said the following:

> "Do you have a large stake in gldcoins? Are you an active supporter of GLDCoins who is interested in trying to help support the currency? Join our skype group and work to be a part of important decisions. These will be decisions about our plans for how to build up GLDCoin not for profit but as a coin and similar things."

A Bitcointalk forum thread was created by user "Kumala" on the 24th of May titled "Vircurex: Which of these coins would you like to see on Vircurex". Besides the thread, an online vote was initiated. After a total of 821 votes had been cast, voting ceased at 17:38:02 UTC on the 31st of May. The top four of ten coin choices were:

> Worldcoin 202; Digitalcoin 199; None of them 165; Goldcoin 79; Phoenixcoin 64

User "just_me" gave 10 GLD to each person who voted for GLDCoin's addition to Vircurex. On the 24th of May at 19:12:33 UTC, the first post by user "akumaburn" on the original official GLDCoin Bitcointalk forum thread was submitted. He said:

> "I think just having "gold" in the name makes this more valuable than the other alt-coin attempts."

In the early hours (UTC) of the 24th of May, GLDCoin trading pairs GLD/BTC and GLD/LTC began to actively trade on the exchange called Cryptsy. This exchange launched on the 20th of May 2013. It was based in Delray Beach, Florida, USA. GLDCoin ceased trading on Cryptsy on the 14th of January 2016 at 22:10:58 EDT. The last trade was a sell of 5.67907097 GLD at 487 Bitcoin Satoshi per one unit of GLD account. The value of one Bitcoin at the time was approximately $428.

At this time, users "akumaburn", "BitshireHashaway", "just_me" and "btceic" were encouraging people to participate and praising the generosity of the community.

On the 26th of May, a significant number of supporters of the coin were concerned about the absence of the founder or developers. Users "akumaburn" and "BitshireHashaway" pledged that they would both be willing to take the helm if need be. At 22:15:40 UTC on the same day, user "akumaburn" said:

> "Cool heads folks, will be taking over development if in fact DEV has quit.
>
> I suspect otherwise, DEV's forum account has likely been hacked."

MAY 2013

During the last week of the month, transactions were taking a very long time (approx. 3-4 hours) to confirm due to an attack on the network protocol by large miners. The network protocol was in a state of low hashing power (hash) and high difficulty until the next re-adjustment of the difficulty could occur. User "gldcoin" on the 27th of May at 05:09:35 UTC was quoted as saying:

> "Making changes? No, we aren't going to hard fork the chain because of the difficulty. Mine the coin, and the difficulty should drop. Block rewards are 500 - this was done so mining was worthwhile even at higher difficulties of 30, 40 , 50, etc Eventually block rewards will only be 100.
>
> You can't just change the difficulty and block times on a whim. You have to hard fork the chain which can lead to disaster."

User "akumaburn" responded to the above at 14:55:56 UTC on the same day:

> "I think a hard fork may be the only option here. The difficulty adjustment times are simply too slow.
>
> You may talk about block rewards offsetting the fact that mining is slow, but traders don't care about that sort of thing.
>
> Spikes in difficulty destroy the profitability of the coin."

A discussion ensued during which time the community began to get worried about the future prospects of the coin. Some members of the community emphasised that the coin was not even one month old, so required time to mature. Others were expecting too much too soon.

On the 28th of May at 22:03:16 UTC, user "gldcoin" was quoted as saying:

> "whoever runs gold coin talk forums better get over there really quick and remove a few threads - I alerted the board to them.
>
> People need to ONLY download the official binaries that I alone post."

On the 28th of May, version 0.6.3.2 of an updated wallet client was released. User "gldcoin" posted the relevant link to this new client update (binaries) on page one of the original GLDCoin Bitcointalk forum thread. Despite opposition from user "gldcoin" to a future hard fork, one would occur at block number 21,000. Cryptsy and pool operators had to download and install this update as soon as possible.

On the last day of the month, the GLD/BTC trading pair was removed from Cryptsy. According to the website www.cryptocoincharts.info, GLD/BTC trading resumed on the 25th August 2013.

Bitcoin Satoshi values of GLDCoin on Cryptsy during the last week of May were:

	Price	Low	Open	Close	High	Volume (GLD)
26th May	1,574.5	101	1,700	1,449	7,000	2,613,926
27th May	1,374	840	1,448	1,300	3,112	2,458,789
28th May	1,318	1,000	1,212	1,424	1,500	1,223,021
29th May	1,108	851	1,310	906	1,447	1,394,806
30th May	727.5	400	950	505	1,049	557,270.8

source: www.cryptocoincharts.info

Other events which occurred in the month of May were:

- On the 19th of May at 18:14:47 UTC, user "BitcoinBoard" created a thread on Bitcointalk titled "[GLD] GLDCoin Giveaway!". Users were encouraged to post their GLD wallet address in order to receive 10 GLD.

- On the 24th of May at 19:22:30 UTC, the www.reddit.com/r/goldcoin Reddit Page was created.

- User "btceic" created another GLD giveaway thread on Bitcointalk titled "Free GLD Coin Give Away". The first 1,000 would receive 5 GLD each who sign up and reply to at least 1 thread at GLDCoinTalk.org forum.

NEW DEVELOPMENT TEAM RESCUED GLDCOIN

JUNE 2013

I.   User "MicroGuy" posted his first comment on the GLDCoin thread.

II. Current official GLDCoin forum went live at www.gldtalk.org.

III. New GLDCoin Bitcointalk forum thread created by user "MicroGuy".

IV. First hard fork kicked in at block number 21,000.

V.   Official website www.gldcoin.com went live.

Discussion resumed about the best course of action to protect the network protocol from attack. There were members who wanted the difficulty re-targeting to reduce from every 504 blocks. Blocks were still taking a very long time to find at a relatively high difficulty. The patience of the community was being tested. On the 2nd of June, user "MicroGuy" posted his first comment on the original GLDCoin Bitcointalk thread. At 02:09:11 UTC, he said the following:

> "If anyone wants to give me a deal, I would like to buy some GLD for BTC."

On the same day at 03:31:59 UTC, user "akumaburn" replied:

> "Check Cryptsy."

Some members of the GLDCoin community became worried after they had noticed the missing links to the wallet client. Once again, a few people questioned whether the coin had been abandoned by the founder/developer "gldcoin". Even user "MicroGuy" asked a question on the 2nd of June at 20:24:30 UTC:

> "Where is best place to download client?"

On the same day at 22:10:02 UTC, user "BitcoinFX" said:

> "Erm... They are ready. ^^
>
> Scanned new gldcoin-0.6.4-win32-setup.exe binaries and they are OK. As in fact were all of the previous 'official' downloads for GLDcoin.
>
> http://virusscan.jotti.org/en/scanresult/49d372d4eba68701b8155ea0fc003e7375ce2f70 OK
>
> https://www.virustotal.com/en/file/0df66f90f405aa163e9081a2c886ece585e391c37824ac665f31b5351f71dd8b/analysis/1370208806/ OK
>
> Seeding again soon.
>
> Also, does anyone know the owner of gld.vircurpool.com ? I set some clients mining at that pool, but its 'lagging' at the moment due to requiring the update. Sent 2 emails already. Might even set-up my own GLDcoin pool if things are going well."

Sixty four seconds later, user "MicroGuy" responded:

> "Thanks. I see the link on page one is working again."

User "MicroGuy" was keen to receive some GLDCoin in order to test the client he had recently downloaded and installed. After he had politely requested a few GLD to test the client, user "Miki77" sent him some. User "MicroGuy" was grateful for receiving his very first GLD.

On the 3rd of June at 01:15:47 UTC, user "MicroGuy" asked another question:

"Can someone do a conversion and tell me the current GLD/USD price?
Math is not my strong suit."

Forty two minutes later, user "BitshireHashaway" answered:

"Around $0.000813271, so you can get around 12.3/penny."

On the 5th of June at 07:17:41 UTC, user "MicroGuy" posted:

"At one time I was very interested in GLD because I truly believe it has a lot of potential in terms of mass appeal. Consumer adoption is key to long term business success and the name Gold Coin does have a nice ring. In my view this coin has the potential of overtaking litecoin as the number two BTC contender as long as all shady elements are removed.

That is why I also find it highly troubling that the administrator/operator of the "official GLD forum" is now a known/confirmed scammer.

https://bitcointalk.org/index.php?topic=225137.0"

Also on the 5th of June, it had become evident that the forum gldcointalk.org (created last month by user "kr4x") had become unavailable. User "BitcoinBoard" was working on a new forum platform for official GLD discussion. Later that day at 14:34:15 UTC, user "BitcoinBoard" was quoted as saying:

"New forums are online, feel free to register: http://gldcoinforum.com

Please ignore the ugly look of the forum atm, as I am going to add some more boards now, create a logo etc"

Ten minutes later, user "BitcoinBoard" went on to say:

> "So, here is the deal: the owner of gldcointalk scammed someone for 500K gldcoins and has closed the forum. This member was also posting on threads that GLDcoin is dead and that he was dumping all his coins. He was also selling the forum to make his last quick buck before he left the GLDCoin community.
>
> I have therefore created a new forum for us which can be found here:
> http://gldcoinforum.com
>
> I have some decent knowledge about PHP, Mysql, CSS and HTML so I will be able to manage this forum correctly. We need a stable website with a supportive admin to build a solid base for the community. I hope I will see you on the GLDCoin forum!
>
> Thanks"

User "AZIZ1977" said he would join the new GLDCoin forum. On the 5th of June at 19:14:52 UTC, user "MicroGuy" made the following announcement:

> "We have decided to build a forum here: http://www.gldtalk.org
>
> This forum will be stored on a dedicated server running Simple Machines. I do not fully understand the motivation, stability, or intentions of the current developers of this coin. But we will begin by assuming "they" want to build, create, and support, a stable and secure consumer friendly coin. A coin that will be the future of digital currency.
> We will begin with this assumption and do have additional funding and a core development team available as needed.
>
> Beginning shortly we will create a new thread with a generous Gold Coin giveaway."

Members of the community questioned which forum would be the official go to place for GLDCoin discussion. Doubt had arisen over who was responsible for the coin's development. User "MicroGuy" sought ideas and suggestions for improvements to www.gldtalk.org. A giveaway of 100 GLD to each of the first twenty people to register was established on the 6th of June. New forum members had to post something interesting/intriguing, not just their wallet address. The first registered member was called "GOLDMINE" on the 6th of June at 14:39:55 UTC.

On the 7th of June, user "BitshireHashaway" insisted that development begin on a GLDCoin Andriod Wallet App. User "MicroGuy" responded at 15:47:12 UTC with the following:

> "That sounds great. And let's get the wallet syncing issues resolved. If I can help, tell me how."

About forty minutes later, user "BitshireHashaway" replied:

> "I think that problem will be improved if not fixed once we hit block 21000 as the difficulty will reset then which I think will help it. Were currently at block 18838, and at our current rate it should be another week, however, the best way to speed this up and fix this is by mining constantly with as much hashing power as you can throw at it. I'm gonna go do more research about an android app, and contact a few people, and I'll be back with what we need."

User "MicroGuy" was willing to donate GLD or BTC as a means to encourage further additional mining hash. Also, user "BitshireHashaway" proposed to donate GLD or BTC to those who successfully found blocks. In response, user "MicroGuy" at 18:20:57 UTC on the 7th of June said:

> "I like your idea about paying miners bonuses for block founds. Let's start there. I have created this thread to gather suggestions and ideas for implementing the program:
>
> http://www.gldtalk.org/index.php?topic=8.0"

On the above www.gldtalk.org thread, user "MicroGuy" said that, in order to support GLD, he would pay miners $8.00/day per 1,000KH/s to mine GLD. The total amount budgeted for this program was initially set to $40.00/day which was expected to result in an additional 5,000 KH/s of hashing power. Later that day, an alternative budget of $125/week was set towards the program (guaranteed for a minimum of eight weeks for a total of $1000 in pay outs).

On the 8th of June, user "MicroGuy" announced he was making his first GLDCoin YouTube video. He asked the community to help put together two "How to Guides". The winning entries would then receive 1,000 GLD each:

- A quick "How to Guide" for downloading and installing the GLD client.

- A quick "How to Guide" for buying GLD on Cryptsy.

On the 9th of June at 16:13:08 UTC, user "MicroGuy" said:

"There is a lot of skepticism surrounding this coin and for good reason.

Based on all the data I have gathered and my 30+ years experience in the computer business, I personally give this coin a 1 in 6 chance of survival. This means that we need the stars to align properly and for all of the key players to become serious and professional in their approach beginning NOW! The shenanigans and name calling of the past are not helpful. If gold coin is to survive I think those representing it must hold themselves to the very highest levels of honesty and integrity. It doesn't matter what you've done in the past, it's never too late to change.

I personally view this coin as a patient in the hospital connected to a vast array of tubes, hoses, and a ventilator. And running around the hospital bed is a group of children laughing and calling the unconscious patient names. The poor patient is still alive but struggling desperately to remain in this three dimensional reality. And if the doctors can't save it, he will be leaving for the cryptocoin afterworld very soon.

What am I doing?

1. Talking with my associates and bringing awareness and investment to the coin.
2. Paying miners to mine until the tubes and hoses can safely be removed.
3. Making how-to guides for downloading the wallet and buying on Cryptsy.
4. Creating a series of Youtube videos to encourage buying the coin on Cryptsy.
5. Building and maintaining a community forum.

So basically, I am trying to save this patient with 110% of my energy. But I can't do it alone and will need a lot of help from seriously dedicated and focused individuals. Like I said previously, if the stars align just right and the universe smiles on us, there is a possibility this coin could achieve fantastic heights.

If we can all pull together and get this coin off life-support and into the mainstream awareness, it is my belief that this coin could be a "real contender"."

On the 11th of June at 12:58:19 UTC, a new official Bitcointalk thread was created for the coin titled "Gold Coin (GLD) Info Thread - The Future of Digital Currency [NEW THREAD]" at https://bitcointalk.org/index.php?topic=231834.0. From now on, it was evident the name of the coin had eventually shifted from GLDCoin to GoldCoin (but both were still being used interchangeably). The original thread for GoldCoin was locked. On the same day at 13:50:09 UTC, user "MicroGuy" received a private message from the founder "gldcoin". This was the following:

> "I would be happy if you guys would manage this coin from here on out. I have too many things (work, family, I'm building a home, etc) to really be on these sites 24/7.
>
> I own the website: gldcoin.com as well if anyone (the community) is interested in purchasing it from me for a fair (nothing insane I assure you) price in gld or btc. I understand at this point if no one does, but if not I will just hold onto it because it will be worth something at least in the future. Thanks for your support.
>
> Let me know any threads that need to be locked etc. I will still assist in development, but mostly it should be relayed through hyoshi as he is on these forums more than I.
>
> Thanks"

User "MicroGuy" wanted to know if anyone had the source code for version 0.6.3 (send it to gldtalk@gmail.com). He was checking to make sure he had the original. Also, he had just paid up all rigging operations through to the 17th of June 2013.

On the 12th of June at 21:53:06 UTC, user "MicroGuy" was quoted as saying:

> "This is to announce that we have just acquired GLDCOIN.COM for potential use as Official Website!
>
> http://www.gldtalk.org/index.php?topic=54.0"

Also on this day, a total of 13,400,000 GLD had been generated via proof of work mining up to and including block number 21,000:

Block #21,000 (Reward 500 GLD) June 12th 2013 at 5:38:12 PM UTC

Arguments continued on the subject of multiple forums for GoldCoin. Users on Bitcointalk wanted to sell the domain www.gldcointalk.org. User "MicroGuy" said:

> "Put it back online and promise to keep it running for at least 3 months and I'll send 5000 GLD when you get it running and you can keep the domain. My only request is that you put an ad up for GLDTalk™."

On the 17th of June at 20:45:19 UTC, user "MicroGuy" posted:

> "Paid hashing will cease tomorrow as the program is no longer needed. This will pull around 6.5 MH/s from the network. The developers and myself will carefully monitor the network and add hashpower back as/if needed.
>
> https://www.gldtalk.org/index.php?topic=8.msg703#msg703"

Two days previously, a Facebook page at https://www.facebook.com/gldtalk was created. News and updates would be posted there. It no longer exists.

On the 20th of June at 12:09:24 UTC, user "akumaburn" said:

> "I think it'd be best if Cryptsy moved it back to the BTC market soon.
>
> The lack of volume in BTC/LTC trades on Cryptsy is holding GLD back atm.
>
> GLD held the spot as #1 in volume of trades before being moved to secondary market.
>
> I understand that this may be seen as a good thing, but forcing people to buy LTC just to buy GLD is a barrier to entry.
>
> Keep your heads cool folks, we are in for a very big rise in price soon."

On the 25th of June at 20:26:49 UTC, user "MicroGuy" said:

> "The official website of Goldcoin is now online: http://www.gldcoin.com"

Thirteen days previously, the domain http://www.gldcoin.com was purchased from the original developer user "gldcoin" for one Bitcoin. Before it went live, user "Sting17" (a forum moderator) constructed the layout and functionality of the site. As the official GoldCoin website, it would serve as the main repository of links and instructions for downloading and using the wallet client.

On the 26th of June, user "MicroGuy" continued to encourage people onto Cryptsy (GLD/LTC) to help with profitability of the coin. There were also plans in the works to begin development of an Android Wallet App. Ultimately, the plan was to get the coin into the hands of the consumer. A client update was scheduled for early July.

On the 26th of June at 21:32:10 UTC, user "MicroGuy" said:

"I had another idea today for the android app.

My idea is to create a place on the official website where users can enter the phone number of their smart phone to receive a deposit of let's say 100 Goldcoins in exchange for downloading the app.

Then we'll have all these people with preloaded wallets looking for ways of trading them and using them as money. They might then begin using them for payments to each other for services like grass cutting or babysitting for example.
The key is to get the coin into circulation.

If we can get the coins into circulation, the marketplaces will follow."

On the 28th of June, the new developers of GoldCoin fell out with the initial founder called "gldcoin". Accusations were made that the coin was only being run by user "MicroGuy". User "akumaburn" refuted these claims by saying there are quite a few people helping to develop GoldCoin and grow the community.

Also on the 28th of June, a GoldCoin Facebook group https://www.facebook.com/groups/gldcoin/ was created. It was created as a social media platform for fans, supporters and developers of the coin to post the latest news, information and updates. However, this group never became very active.

On the 28th of June at 23:52:27 UTC, user "MicroGuy" responded to user "bitcoin-world.de" who asked ["Hello whats up with the founder of GLD ? He was kicked by you ? Whats up with the future of GLD ?"] by saying:

"Great question!

The last dev sold us the GLD domain for 1BTC because he did not have enough time to work on the project. He was not "kicked".

Then he was paid another 1BTC under the alias of Hyoshi for doing dev work for the community. Of course at the time we did not know that these two people were in fact a single individual using (at minimum) triple identities. Basically he was getting paid left and right while operating under different assumed names. Then while using this Hyoshi alias (he's also apparently thekidcoin) he again indicated in a public post that he didn't have time to work on the project:
https://www.gldtalk.org/index.php?topic=63.msg923#msg923

It was after that statement that we realized for sure we needed to secure additional developers if we wanted a stable and reliable team. The good news is I now believe to know the real life identity of this individual who is being sought by other interested parties. I am currently refusing to participate in the prosecution of this individual but must admit my patience is wearing thin.

We have now assembled a solid reliable dev team of three professionals led by akumaburn and will be releasing a fork soon. The fork will fix several bugs including the litecoin alert, the client sync issue, and the coin generation bug. The fix will also reduce annual coin output and cap supply.
You can read more about the upcoming update here:
https://www.gldtalk.org/index.php?topic=157.0

Rest assured we are working day and night for the betterment of this coin. Thank you and I hope this helps answer your questions."

At the end of June, the network protocol hash was beginning to look healthier due to an increasing number of miners. In addition to this, further promotions of the coin were been initiated to introduce GoldCoin to a wider audience and as a means to increase the circulation of the cryptocurrency. User "MicroGuy" emphasised that promotions help to ultimately grow acceptance and adoption.

Other events which occurred in the month of June were:

- In early June, user "dubs" was supporting the original GoldCoin forum at http://www.gldcointalk.org. It was viewed by some as being very active before it became unavailable on the 5th of June 2013.

- On the 12th of June, user "RichG" on www.gldtalk.org registered #goldcoin-otc at Freenode.

- On the 13th of June, an independent article was published by "GoldMine" titled "The Price of GLDcoins is trending up in June 2013". This ascent in value against Litecoin can be seen in the graphic below.

- User "MicroGuy" created an email address contact@gldcoin.com for communicating official messages, important announcements, and client release alerts. He announced this on gldtalk.org on the 23rd of June.

- On the 25th of June, user "Sting17" on gldtalk.org offered his services for Graphic Design to create logos, business cards, website graphics etc. He was willing to receive payment in Bitcoin, Litecoin and, obviously, GoldCoin.

- On the 30th of June, user "tadspoles" on gldtalk.org suggested marketing GoldCoin to some places such as actual gold sellers. User "akumaburn" recommended this sort of marketing after the next wallet client update to be released soon next month.

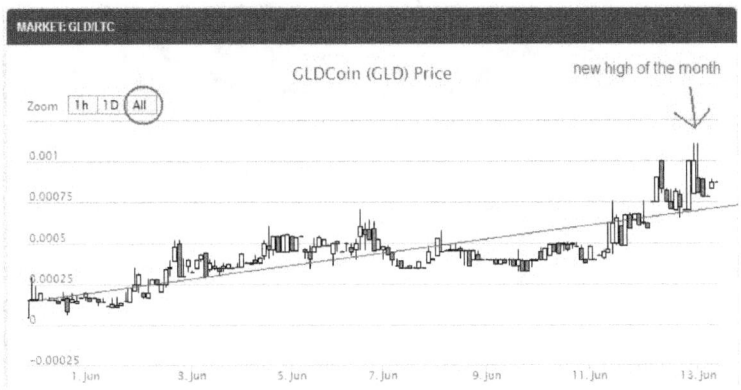

VERSION 1.2 OF THE WALLET CLIENT RELEASED

JULY 2013

I.   Decision made to reduce the block reward and the re-targeting time.

II.   Lowest market capitalisation of GoldCoin in 2013 recorded.

III.   New official GoldCoin logo unveiled thanks to user "Sting17".

IV.   Version 1.2 update of the wallet client released.

V.   What makes GoldCoin different? Why is it better?

Testing of a new wallet client was still in progress. The lead developer, user "akumaburn", said he had been working tirelessly for about three days straight.

At this time, user "MicroGuy" was publishing YouTube videos in which he discussed the coin and other cryptocurrency news. His aim was to reach an audience of people outside the sphere of the "crypto-world". A few users on Bitcointalk said he was not taking criticism well. In a sense, he was attempting to give the coin a fun, light-hearted and entertaining slant, but some thought he was not being professional or serious enough. User "MicroGuy" said:

> "I am trying to learn to take criticism better. I just removed all my videos from this thread per the suggestion above. In addition, I will delete any future video that does not have an overwhelming majority of likes vs. dislikes."

According to www.cryptocoincharts.info, the value of one unit of GLD account had been decreasing everyday from the 16th of June to the first day of July. During this period, the value decreased from 0.00084355 GLD/LTC to 0.000150535 GLD/LTC. This would actually be close to the lowest LTC value on Cryptsy (0.00014327 LTC or $0.0003624731 per GLD on 8th July) for the year 2013.

On the 2nd of July at 11:38:57 UTC, user "MicroGuy" said:

"Good morning everyone!

One of the coins currently being traded at Cryptsy could well become the currency of the future.

It will be the one that is ultimately adopted by consumers that will succeed. So focusing on fixing the client and then getting this currency into circulation is paramount. My idea is to have a series of television commercials showing people in the future using Goldcoins in their everyday life. In one version a female jogger tips the paper wallet of a sleeping homeless man then comes home and pays the babysitter by sending coins to her smartphone.

Over the coming weeks we will be announcing a contest and will begin accepting video commercial submissions. The winner will receive a cash bonus and could have his/her entry featured on late night television in select cities.

Have a great day guys and "may all your bitcoin dreams turn to gold"!"

Two days later at 13:17:25 UTC, user "MicroGuy" said:

"The updated client will be released in a few days. Thank you for your patience."

On the 5th of July, a change of the difficulty re-targeting period to every 60 blocks was decided.

On the following day, the upcoming new wallet client was being rigorously tested on a private testnet. It would be released once they were confident of it functioning properly.

On the 7th of July at 00:48:40 UTC, user "coinerer" posted the following:

"This is from Readme.md
https://github.com/goldcoin/gldcoin/blob/master/README.md on date 7th of July 2013.

GoldCoin (GLD) - an improved version of Litecoin using scrypt as a proof of work scheme.

2.5 minute block targets up till block 30500
2 minute block targets there after
504 blocks per difficulty retarget up to block 30500
60 blocks per difficulty retarget thereafter
Block rewards in order:
200 Block @ 10000 GLD
2000 Blocks @ 1000 GLD
24000 Blocks @ 500 GLD
262800 Blocks @ 400 GLD ...
262800 Blocks @ 8 GLD
Total Blocks: 26310500
The default ports are 8121 (connect) and 8122 (fson rpc)

I hope they would leave unchanged total number of coins from this data:
about 123 millions."

On the 7th of July at 14:22:33 UTC, user "MicroGuy" said:

"The repository is in the process of being updated.

As stated previously, we inherited the current client distribution and are working to repair it in regards to the client sync issues, litecoin alert message, and infinite coin generation. Currently the coin generation rules are "stuck" at a block reward of 500 for infinity. This is something we inherited and are working to resolve in a manner that will bring long-term viability to the coin. The new rules will have a gradual reduction of block reward and a cap on total coin output after an extended period of time.

Anyone interested in actually contributing to the project is welcome to register for the forum and participate in the discussion including the member's only section which is not viewable to the outside World.

Thanks for everyone who is supporting Goldcoin!

The future is looking brighter and brighter!"

On the 7th of July at 16:48:25 UTC, user "MicroGuy" said:

"Yes. We are reducing the block reward to 400 at the fork and then beginning a gradual block reward reduction over an extended period. The github does not contain all the updated code or readme's but will be updated soon.

The last obstacle in terms of coding is the migration from litecoin to our own prefix.

We need to be able to:

- Read the prefork prefix wallet and block databases with the new client.
- Write the database with all prefork blocks with the earlier prefix, but the postfork blocks with the new prefix.
- Have the client be able to trade with both sets of prefixes but only accept the prefork prefix for blocks that are earlier than "julyFork".
- Accept connections from clients that are using the prefork prefix if and only if their blockheight is less than "julyFork".
- Accept connections from all new clients and propagate block changes throughout the network successfully.

Once we have found the best solution (suggestions are welcome) to this problem and tested its functionality, we will publish and release the update."

On the 9th of July, user "Sting17" at 13:22:51 UTC said:

"Like MicroGuy has said we are working extremely hard to iron out all the bugs to do with removing the lite coin prefix. We have finalised a coin generation plan and hope to launch all details and new client very soon.

We will not release this until we are 100% satisfied. Everyone in the Gold Team thanks everyone for their patience."

Also on the 9th of July, the lowest market capitalisation (the overall US Dollar value of all GLD mined to date) was recorded at about $5,143. A corresponding Bitcoin Satoshi value of 359 per unit account of GLD was evident. It was important to note that GLD was only actively trading on Cryptsy at the time, so all data attaining to these figures was derived from there.

On the 19th of July at 22:47:50 UTC, user "MicroGuy" unveiled the new official GoldCoin logo. He submitted the following post on the www.gldtalk.org forum:

Two comments on the official GoldCoin Bitcointalk thread (second thread) were posted by two users on the 23rd of July. Firstly, user "amytheplanarshift" said:

"That new logo looks really nice!"

Secondly, user "seleme" said:

"yep, nice logo"

Discussion about GoldCoin was beginning to shift from the second official GoldCoin Bitcointalk forum thread to the official forum at www.gldtalk.org.

JULY 2013

On the 27th of July at 15:11:15 UTC, user "MicroGuy" posted the following announcement. It was the release of version 1.2 of the wallet client:

> "We are proud to announce the latest update to GoldCoin.
>
> The development team and staff have been working around the clock to make this the very best version to date.
>
> We have addressed a number of issues related to the previous client. The syncing issues and Litecoin upgrade alert have been fixed. In addition, there have been improvements made in the areas of coin generation, block reward, and difficulty retarget time.
>
> For a more in depth look at the changes and an explanation regarding those changes, please take a look at the official patch documentation here:
>
> http://www.gldcoin.com/documents/GoldCoin_Patch_v1.2.pdf
>
> There will be a hard-fork at block 45000 which is currently estimated to occur on August 1, 2013. All current users should update their clients at least 24 hours prior to the fork. It is recommended that you backup your current wallet before performing this upgrade.
>
> To update your client please visit the official website and select the version of the client that matches your operating system: http://www.gldcoin.com
>
> Join the discussion at GLDTalk.org: https://www.gldtalk.org/index.php?topic=221.0"

As discussed in the first official GoldCoin Patch Announcement, the development team had been working tirelessly for the last six weeks. At block number 21,000, the first hard fork in the GoldCoin blockchain occurred. Either by accident or on purpose, the limit on coins to be generated ceased to exist and the coin generation rules became void. A reward per block of 500 GLD existed indefinitely.

A new coin limit of 123,423,900 (to be mined over one hundred years) was chosen. Other coin specification changes starting at block number 45,000 would be:

- Block time reduced from 2.5 minutes to 2 minutes.
- Difficulty re-targeting time reduced from 504 blocks to 60 blocks.
- Block reward reduced from 500 GLD to 45 GLD.

During the month of July, user "MicroGuy" posted the following about his opinion on "What makes GoldCoin different? Why is it better?". He said:

"There have been a few times on the main bitcointalk thread where people have asked, "What makes Goldcoin different? What makes it better than the other coins?". So I had some extra time this morning and decided to write this post.

Discovery: In late March of this year, I started hearing about this digital currency called "bitcoin". I then started researching and learning about it and many other alt coins including litecoin. At some point I began seeing some limitations in these coins that needed to be addressed. It was about this time that I found out about Goldcoin. At the time I became involved the coin was near death and needed to have artificial life support in the way of paid mining to support the network hash rate. The coin has now been resuscitated and is breathing on its own thanks to a wonderful community and talented team of developers and forum staff.

Rebulding: The next step is to repair the client which needs a major overhaul. This must be done with much consideration as we attempt to balance "protecting current investors" against "improving the coin with a hard fork". Since the market price currently reflects a view that the coin is dead, anything that we do to keep the coin alive and give it a chance to thrive will protect current investors. So now we are in the process of giving this coin a complete makeover and are working to overcome one last technical obstacle which involves fixing a flaw in the original design. For more information on this technical issue go here: https://bitcointalk.org/index.php?topic=251907.0.

Once we complete testing and release the updated client, Goldcoin will not only have a chance to survive, it will have a great opportunity for sustained universal success!

I guess that's about all for now. Thanks to the many many people currently working to make Goldcoin a success!"

At the end of the month, there were calls for Cryptsy to bring back the direct GLD/BTC trading pair to their exchange platform. On the 31st of July at 15:49:38 UTC, user "AZIZ1977" was quoted as saying:

"We need to have a big rise in volume, price and new supporters so that it can be used as arguments to get Goldcoin back in BTC market. When thats accomplished then we start lobbying at BTC-e to add us."

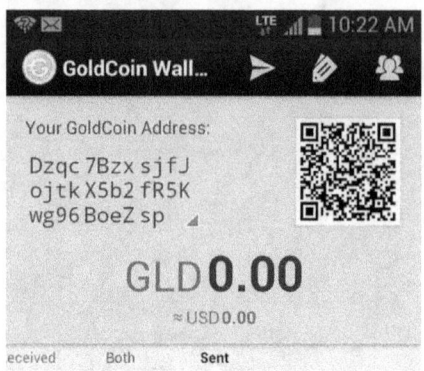

No GoldCoin sent so far.

GOLDCOIN ANDROID WALLET APP RELEASED

AUGUST 2013

I.   The second hard fork kicked in at block number 45,000.

II.   Value of one unit of GLD account surged over $0.01.

III.   GoldCoin began to trade on the exchange called CoinEX.

IV.   GLD/BTC and GLD/LTC markets simultaneously active on Cryptsy again.

V.   GoldCoin Android Wallet App released.

The community were anticipating the second hard fork of the GoldCoin blockchain at block number 45,000. User "Stouse49" at several preceding block numbers attempted to estimate the time of this block.

Also at the beginning of the month, user "AZIZ1977" created a GoldCoinInfo Twitter page at https://twitter.com/GoldCoinInfo to inform people about and promote GoldCoin socially. It ceased operations on the 10th of December 2015.

At block number 44,999, a total of 25,399,500 GLD had been mined:

Block #44,999 (Reward 500 GLD) August 2nd 2013 at 08:11:19 AM UTC

Block #45,000 (Reward 45 GLD) August 2nd 2013 at 08:13:50 AM UTC

On the 2nd of August at 18:10:01 UTC, user "tadspoles" said:

> "Methinks we need that Android Client sooner than imagined. Good job the developers.
>
> GoldCoin is most definitely BACK on it's original growth path now!"

On the 3rd of August, the price of one unit of GLD account peaked at the highest value so far at 0.001109445 LTC on Cryptsy. In terms of USD, the price had increased from $0.000362 to $0.00296 since the 8th of July. This was an increase of 700-800% in the space of less than one month.

Two days later, user "Sting17" said that an Android Wallet App was in progress. At the time, a professional and experienced developer was being sought after.

On the 6th of August, user "RichG" created another GoldCoin Twitter page at https://twitter.com/gldcoin. It was evident that three Twitter accounts existed for GoldCoin without prior collaboration. Members of the community enquired whether they should all merge into a new official account for the coin.

> https://twitter.com/GoldcoinGLD
> https://twitter.com/gldcoin (created by user "RichG")
> https://twitter.com/GoldCoinInfo (created by user "AZIZ1977")

On the 6th of August at 15:06:24 UTC, user "akumaburn" said:

> "We will be having a non-mandatory update this week so stay tuned."

This new non-mandatory wallet client would include only cosmetic changes such as QR code support.

On the 9th of August at 16:44:30 UTC, user "akumaburn" said:

> "Mac client incoming (standalone version) as well as support for QR codes."

On the 13th of August at 14:30:00 UTC, user "akumaburn" said:

> "Support for QR codes added, however there still appear to be issues with the Mac client, we are working to resolve this.
>
> New: We are working on an android client."

On the 14th of August, a sneak preview of the new Android App was published (see page 66). Members of the community were asking for an estimated time of release and some were willing to help and support its continued development. The developers anticipated it would be ready for release within one month.

On the 16th of August, user "MicroGuy" said:

> "Here's a look at the new app as it appears on my Samsung Galaxy phone."

On the 17th of August at 01:39:41 UTC, user "MicroGuy" said:

> "The upcoming GoldCoin Android App was under development when the Android Security Vulnerability described here
> (http://bitcoin.org/en/alert/2013-08-11-android) was published.
>
> The fix that was then added by Andreas Schildbach on August 11 to the Bitcoin Android Wallet (https://github.com/schildbach/bitcoin-wallet) was applied to the GoldCoin app.
>
> The new random number generation implementation was verified to be in use by the GoldCoin App when creating new addresses."

On the 19th of August, www.gldtalk.org user "ipaint" announced the following:

> "8/19/2013: (1) One GLD/USD $0.01252 | 79.89266249 Goldcoins Per US Dollar 😃 YES!!! We hit 1 cent!!! Now lets see how high it can go."

On the 21st of August at 19:39:48 UTC, user "erundook" said:

> "Gold Coin is added to https://coinex.pw exchange & mining pool."

On the same day at 22:52:45 UTC, user "akumaburn" said:

> "Awesome, but we should be in BTC section.. the only reason we were moved to LTC section on cryptsy was because we had the highest volume at the time and they wanted to bring that volume to their LTC markets.
>
> We still have thousands of dollars worth of transactions occurring on a daily basis."

After the above comment about GoldCoin being restricted solely to direct trading with Litecoin, CoinEx added the GLD/BTC trading pair to their platform. User "MicroGuy" was quoted as saying:

> "This is welcome news! I have now added your exchange and pool to the OP of this thread. Thank you."

On the 23rd of August, beta testing of the GoldCoin Android Wallet App began. Only those part of the "Twilight Zone" (a members only forum) on www.gldtalk.org could access the download link at this time. The first twenty members of the "Twilight Zone" would receive 200 GLD by being a beta tester.

On the 25th of August at 01:15:08 UTC, user "MicroGuy" said:

> "Goldcoin (GLD) is now traded on both the BTC and LTC markets at Crytpsy.com!
>
> https://www.gldtalk.org/index.php?topic=347.0
>
> Thanks to BitJohn, BigVern, and the entire crew at Cryptsy for this new dual listing status!"

On the 27th of August at 23:04:13 UTC, user "MicroGuy" said:

> "Yes. There's a lot of exciting announcements coming soon including the public release of the new Android App!" 😃

On the following day, user "MicroGuy" said he had recently installed an advertising package on the official forum. No adverts existed as of yet, but his idea was to position advertisements in selected parts of the forum for websites that accept GLD as a form of payment.

On the 31st of August at 02:54:48 UTC, user "MicroGuy" said:

> "Yes! It's finally here, the new Goldcoin™ mobile Android App for your Smart phone!
>
> Now you can take your Goldcoins on the road and exchange them with family and friends on the go. Use them to pay your child for babysitting or for washing the family car. Teach them the value of money and how to track their investment as it grows. But most of all have fun!"

A giveaway was established to celebrate the release of the new Android Wallet App. The first twenty people to post a screenshot of their App would receive 200 GLD in the wallet address shown in that screenshot (see page 66)

Other events which occurred in the month of August were:

- On the 5th of August, user "Stouse49" submitted instructions on www.gldtalk.org about how to install the GoldCoin wallet client on Windows (XP, Vista, 7 and 8) and Mac (Linux still awaiting addition).

- On the 13th of August, user "MicroGuy" welcomed Zuck to the team as Linux Systems Engineer in one of his YouTube videos.

- On the 20th of August, user "Stouse49" submitted a guide on www.gldtalk.org about how to mine . He described the mining hardware, pools and methods available.

GOLDCOIN ANDROID WALLET APP RELEASED ON THE GOOGLE PLAY STORE

SEPTEMBER 2013

I.   Technical problems for European users of the Android Wallet App reported.

II.   GoldCoin added to the list of supported coins at www.coinpayments.net.

III.   A new GoldCoin faucet released at http://goldcoinfaucet.com/.

IV.   User "MicroGuy" advertised two paid positions within the community.

V.   GoldCoin Android Wallet App now available on Google Play Store.

Many supporters and participants in GoldCoin were happy to see the release of the Android Wallet App. However, one user at the end of August notified the developers of a fault. User "bitcoin-world.de" said his installed GoldCoin Android Wallet App was crashing on his Samsung Galaxy Tab3. On the 1st of September at 00:13:29 UTC, user "MicroGuy" replied:

> "We appreciate your valuable feedback.
>
> The app developer has isolated this issue and found it to be related to the way the App does European decimal formatting. The problem will be fixed and an update released in the next two to three days. Users in the United States are not affected by this issue.
>
> Thank you again for bringing this to our attention."

On the 2nd of September at 06:17:23 UTC, user "MicroGuy" said:

"I've just been informed that voting is underway to determine if CoinPayments.net decides to begin supporting Goldcoin (GLD).

Please vote now >> https://bitcointalk.org/index.php?topic=286120.0

You can help by placing your vote now and telling other Goldcoin enthusiasts about this Golden voting opportunity!"

Here was an inexhausive list of where GLD was going to be accepted if added:

Daily Deals - http://www.dailybit.net
Bet on LTC to GOX & Coinbase! - http://www.LitecoinToGox.com
Win a PS4! - http://www.Playstation4Raffle.com
Car parts, games, and more! - http://www.mtyimport.com
Gift Shop - http://orbitcoin.org
Prepaid Visa Cards - http://www.visa4crypto.com
Poor College Girls Store - http://www.poorcollegegirls.com/store
Order Gold & Silver - http://iGotSpots.com/other.html
Frontier Space - http://www.frontier-space.com/frontiercart/
Mining Supplies - https://coincable.com/
Prepaid Phone Cards , Pay Utility Bills & More - http://cryptopcs.com/

On the 3rd of September at 10:39:32 UTC, user "MicroGuy" said:

"Goldcoin has been added to https://CoinPayments.net list of supported coins: https://www.gldtalk.org/index.php?topic=414.0

A special thanks to CoinPayments and everyone who voted."

CoinPayments provide an easy to integrate checkout system (multi crypto coin payment processing system) for cryptocurrencies such as Bitcoin and Litecoin with low fees. Initial coins added were BTC, LTC, DVC, CGB, BQC, FTC, IFC, KGC, NMC, NVC, ORB, RED, STR, TRC, XPM, PPC, CAP, YAC, DGC, GLD and WDC.

On the 3rd of September at 21:06:32 UTC, user "MicroGuy" said:

"Update Notice

The development team has just published a non-forking security update to the client that adds extra checkpoints. Notice for non-windows users: The GLDCoin directory has been renamed to GoldCoin (GLD), you will have to move your wallet file manually. As always for all users, we recommend taking a backup of your wallet.dat file.

You can download the latest update here: http://gldcoin.com/get-started/

If you have any problems installing the latest update, you can get assistance directly from the developers in our new support forum:https://www.gldtalk.org/index.php?board=22.0

We are also pleased to announce a new Goldcoin faucet: http://goldcoinfaucet.com/"

On the 7th of September, user "bitcoin-world.de" was waiting for the fixed GoldCoin Android App to be uploaded to the Google Play Store. He wanted to show a fully functioning application to his family and friends, hence grow community participation. On the same day at 15:45:27 UTC, user "MicroGuy" said:

"Thanks for your support!

The update to the Android App was released a couple of days ago and can be downloaded below:

http://gldcoin.com/get-started/

Also new users will receive 200GLD by posting a screenshot of their app in this thread:

https://www.gldtalk.org/index.php?topic=403.0"

On the 21st of September at 03:58:22 UTC, user "MicroGuy" encouraged members of the community, especially people who had been part of it since the beginning, to help make newbies on www.gldtalk.org welcome. User "MicroGuy" did not want to be seen as the only person doing so. He went onto say:

> "I'm going to make this is a sticky topic because it's important and everyone should try it! When you see a new member post in the newbie section simply say hello and welcome them to the forum.
>
> You might even offer to help them with any questions!"

On the following day at 06:29:25 UTC, user "Stouse49" was happy to point out that GoldCoin had sustained its position on Cryptsy on both the Bitcoin and Litecoin trading markets, despite other coins soon to be removed. He said:

> "September 21, 2013
>
> Today BigVern @cryptsy announced that the HYC, CNC, CRC, NAN, GIL Markets will be closing on OCT 1st. This is "Due to inactive developers and low hashrates, this coin will be delisted from the market on Oct 1st, 2013. Wallets will remain open indefinately."
>
> This is the first time to my knowledge that coins are being delisted, since Powercoin (which was 51% attacked). There have been times when certain coins were removed from trading temporarily due to various problems with those coins.
> ChinaCoin (CNC) was the oldest of these coins that will be delisted.
>
> Additionally, WDC and DGC are now in both BTC and LTC markets. This status was first achieved by GoldCoin in May of 2013."

On the 23rd of September, user "MicroGuy" advertised two paid positions within the community. One of these was a "Social Media Specialist" who would keep all social media sites updated with links to the newest GoldCoin information (software updates, new services, new pools, etc). The other position was for an experienced "Chinese Translator" who would translate text for the client and the Android Wallet App as well as, perhaps, write how-to guides on gldtalk.org and gldcoin.com.

On the 24th of September at 04:21:43 UTC, user "MicroGuy" said:

"We're very pleased to announce that the Goldcoin (GLD) Android App is now available for download on the Google Play Store. This makes downloading the app and sharing Goldcoins with friends and family a breeze!

https://play.google.com/store/apps/details?id=de.schildbach.wallet.goldcoin&hl=en

Website download:

http://gldcoin.com/get-started/

In addition the Goldcoin Android app is MIT open source and available for free here:

https://github.com/goldcoin/goldcoin-android

A special thanks goes out to the developer Stouse49 for all his work coding and publishing the Android wallet. This achievement would not have been possible without his dedicated efforts."

51% DEFENSE ALGORITHM

OCTOBER 2013

I.   Article titled "GoldCoin: The Scam That Keeps On Giving" published.

II. Mandatory wallet client version 0.7 released.

III. Mandatory wallet client version 0.7.1 released.

IV. A new (third) GoldCoin Bitcointalk forum thread created.

V.   Block number 100,000 reached (new 51% defence system).

An opportunity was given to members of the community to create a video commercial for GoldCoin, which could then be uploaded to YouTube. An undisclosed reward of GLD would then be paid to talented "videomakers". In addition, there was a GLD giveaway to celebrate the recent Android Wallet release. Bitcointalk users had to make their avatar GoldCoin related to qualify. In accordance with this, on the 2nd of October at 15:48:50 UTC, user "MicroGuy" said:

> "To celebrate the brand new Goldcoin Wallet App (now available in Google Play Store) we're giving away a ton of gold!
>
> https://bitcointalk.org/index.php?topic=303535.0
>
> Be sure to stayed tuned for our big Indiegogo announcement coming soon!"

On the 2nd of October at 15:15:10 UTC, user "Hazard" was quoted as saying:

> "Daily reminder that GLDCoin is a scam, and your money is better invested elsewhere:
>
> http://cryptolife.net/goldcoin-the-scam-that-keeps-on-giving"

In the article titled "GoldCoin: The Scam That Keeps On Giving", user "Hazard" described how the coin was initially mined by the founders at low difficulty and at disproportionately high block rewards. He described user "MicroGuy" as a "con man" who relaunched the coin, stockpiled GLD and then sought to reduce the block reward to increase the value of his own holdings. The end of the article was:

> "Goldcoin represents everything that is bad about the world of alternate cryptocurrency. It is spearheaded by an individual who cares about nothing other than lining his own pockets. There is not one redeeming factor about this coin; it's the purest example of a scamcoin to date. Your money is better invested elsewhere."

User "MicroGuy" was, to a moderate extent, surprised that anyone would take the article seriously. He viewed it as an attack on himself and the community as a whole. He emphasised that his investment in the GoldCoin project far exceeded the value of his GLD holdings. What was more important to him was his interest in its long term growth and potential. He concluded his response by saying:

> "I honesty believe in the future of this coin and its chances of making the top-three in terms of marketcap. We have a terrific name, a dedicated development team, and a hard-working loyal community.
>
> I'd like to take this opportunity to thank everyone for supporting Goldcoin!
>
> We genuinely appreciate your support!"

Users "akumaburn" and "kelsey also defended GoldCoin against the accusations made by user "Hazard". They thought it was a blatant attempt to discredit GoldCoin.

On the 10th of October at 18:36:24 UTC, user "AZIZ1977" said:

> "What i like about the Goldcoin is that community is very dedicated to making GLD a success. Even when people tried and still are trying to bash GLD to the ground the Goldcoin community always stood as a rock behind the coin and made the coin even stronger than it was a couple months ago. To be honest even if you had the best innovative crypto currency if you dont have a loyal dedicated community the coin will be doomed. GLD community knows that to be successful we need to attract also the average guy who isn't in crypto."

On the 10th of October at 18:51:11 UTC, user "MicroGuy" said:

> "There are several differences that you can investigate by reading the various technical materials. The code is under constant development. We will also be soon releasing a 51% defense that will be a first in the entire industry.
>
> Keep in mind however that the consumer has very little interest in technical differences and is more sensitive to branding and appearance. You can observe this in brand-named items vs their generic counter-parts. You can make a highly functional shoe that's nearly identical to a major brand and the consumer will pay 4X or 5X more for a name like Nike. The consumer isn't as concerned with "differences" as much as they are the name and logo. And in my consumer testing the name "Goldcoin" scores the highest among all altcoins in terms of overall desirability.
>
> But I would also remind the reader that this coin is in its infancy at just a little over 4 months old and is not a "static" thing. The coin is rapidly growing and evolving, and as it grows and evolves it's becomes more unique and more different as it develops its own identity.
>
> And we as a community are here to help it along its way and nurture it as it grows into a blossoming flower."

On the same day, user "AZIZ1977" suggested it would be a great idea in the future to send an automatic e-mail to all forum members in order to notify them of a wallet client update. Another person said people should visit the forum regularly to keep informed of the latest developments. User "MicroGuy" said a new alert system is being tested and will be implemented for use in the next update.

On the 11th of October at 23:25:40 UTC, user "akumaburn" said:

"GoldCoin v0.7 Released! Mandatory soft-forking update!

Download here: http://gldcoin.com/get-started/

New release is 51% resistant and multipool proof!

51% attack proof past block 100,000! (Mass IP farms aside)

For those who didn't know: GLD is Proof of WORK! not POS

First proof of work coin to do this.

Read about it here:
http://gldcoin.com/documents/GoldCoin_0.7_51percent_defense_october_11_2013.pdf"

The developers emphasised the importance of this latest wallet client update. As more users update, the more secure the entire GoldCoin network protocol will be from attack (see the appendix on pages 135 to 137).

On the 19th of October, an opinion was publically posted about alt-coins:

"I think in the future we will definitely have multiple alt-coins
being accepted by merchants."

On the 19th of October at 05:05:20 UTC, user "MicroGuy" responded:

"I agree with this statement. I also think it will be the coins with the best "brandablity" and overall consumer appeal that will battle for the top positions. Of course a solid development team backed by a diverse and thriving community will be essential to any successful crypto currency.

It is truly amazing how far Goldcoin has come over the past few months, and we've only

just begun."

On the 19th of October, www.gldtalk.org forum user "AlexBoyle" thanked user "AZIZ1977" for introducing him to GoldCoin. He also described the community as forward thinking and listed the following:

- Creating a coin that is specifically designed for ground level adoption and most importantly getting newbies specifically involved.

- A continual presence on forums and a willingness to help.

- Strong marketing and development pushing the coin forward.

- The name of this coin, how pertinent it is to people and the world market in general.

- Technical development to protect users.

On the 21st of October at 02:28:12 UTC, user "MicroGuy" said:

> "GoldCoin (GLD) Mandatory Update: V 0.7.1
>
> The DevTeam has just published mandatory Goldcoin (GLD) update version 0.7.1. This patch includes improvements to our new defense system released last week.
>
> Download links: http://gldcoin.com/get-started/
>
> Forum announcement: https://www.gldtalk.org/index.php?topic=618.0
>
> The development team is currently on standby in the event you require technical assistance."

On the 24th of October at 11:49:12 UTC, a comment was made by user "Xanis" on the official GoldCoin Bitcointalk forum thread. He said GLD had been quiet for some time now. User "AZIZ1977" responded about six minutes later:

> "GLD is hard working on reaching non crypto people & its slowly working Goldcoin forum is receiving every day new members."

On the 24th of October at 21:39:39 UTC, user "MicroGuy" submitted the final post of the second GoldCoin Bitcointalk forum thread:

> "Please visit the new official GoldCoin Thread:
> https://bitcointalk.org/index.php?topic=317568.0"

This was the third official GoldCoin thread created on the Bitcointalk forum and was titled "GoldCoin™ (GLD) Thread - The Gold Standard of Digital Currency [OFFICIAL THREAD]". The thread was created on the 24th of October at 21:37:51 UTC. It has been the current official thread on there for over two years, but very little discussion occurs on it. The vast majority of discussion takes place at www.gldtalk.org (the official GoldCoin Forum). It has been active since the 5th of June 2013.

On the 25th of October at 16:04:03 UTC, user "akumaburn" said:

> "A new thread makes sense I guess, so much nonsense in the old thread, it's going to be good to have a thread filled only with relevant information.
>
> Ps: I'm not a great fan of self-moderated topics, but at least it will keep those trolls at bay or at least stop them from spamming our thread.
>
> I'll be posting some more information here as time goes by."

On the 27th of October at 13:13:03 UTC on www.gldtalk.org, user "AZIZ1977" proposed the following:

> "Using the Goldcoin logo as avatar on the bitcointalk forum and other crypto forums is a good way of promoting Goldcoin. I urge our Goldcoin miners to change their avatar."
>
> "small acts when multiplied by millions of people can transform the world"

Block #100,000 (Reward 45 GLD) October 31st 2013 at 08:59:56 PM UTC

As can be seen above, the new 51% attack defence code kicked in at block number 100,000. A total of approximately 27,874,545 GLD had been mined/generated up to this point.

Other events which occurred in the month of October were:

- On the 12th of October, user "AZIZ1977" announced that http://btcpipeshop.com had begun accepting GLD as a payment method. The Pipe Shop is a boutique market stall at music festivals around Australia. They accept all methods of digital currency present on www.coinpayments.net.

- On the 14th of October, www.gldtalk.org user "coinman1980" wanted to sell 1.5 million GLD to somebody directly without crashing the price on the market. He initially wanted 40 BTC in exchange. It is unknown whether they were all sold or not.

- User "AZIZ1977" proposed the design. and eventual manufacture. of GoldCoin T-shirts which could then be marketed and sent out free to different big crypto magazines or companies. He made this proposal on the 24th of October on the official GoldCoin forum at www.gldtalk.org.

Your GLD is now SAFE from 51% attacks

FIXES TO THE 51% DEFENSE ALGORITHM
TESTED AND IMPLEMENTED
NOVEMBER 2013

I.   Problems with mining after block number 100,000.

II.   Five wallet client updates released (v 0.7.1.2 to v0.7.1.6).

III. Android Wallet App now compatible with the GoldCoin 51% Defense System.

IV.   Market capitalisation surpassed $1 million for the first time.

V.   A surge in the value of GLD during the last week of the month.

Questions were being asked why the successful mining of GoldCoin was not occurring (rejected coin blocks). Some thought a fork in the blockchain had taken place. User "akumaburn" had been investigating the issue for many hours and decided a new client update was required in order to move forward.

On the 2nd of November at 05:38:18 UTC, user "MicroGuy" responded to the issues/problems that had arisen:

"Yes, part of this is related to the 51% attack defense. However there are still some questions that need to be answered regarding the pools and the blockchain.

The DevTeam is in the process of completing their investigation into this issue and will be making some recommendations in a few hours which will include confirmation of the official chain height and whether a maintenance patch will be needed/released."

On the 2nd of November at 21:27:07 UTC, user "MicroGuy" said the following:

> "The Goldcoin development team has just released mandatory software update V 0.7.1.2.
>
> This update is designed to correct network chain fragmentation caused by a bug in the previous version.
>
> Download links: http://gldcoin.com/get-started/
>
> Support forum: https://www.gldtalk.org/index.php?board=22.0
>
> The development team is currently on standby in the event you require technical assistance."

Wallet client users were advised to verify they were on the correct blockchain by referring to the block explorer at http://gld.cryptocoinexplorer.com/chain/ Goldcoin. There were also instances of people being unable to sync to the blockchain (fully download the blockchain onto their personal computers). The developers said it was taking approximately twenty four hours for this to occur properly. All mining pools were down at this time.

On the 3rd of November at 05:15:41 UTC, user "MicroGuy" informed the community of another upcoming updated wallet client:

> "A new update is being compiled and will be uploaded to the website within the hour.
>
> It's version 0.7.1.3.
>
> http://gldcoin.com/get-started/
>
> I'm running the default config and my client appears to be working properly."

As soon as it was released, everyone had to update to version 0.7.1.3. If any users were experiencing disappearing transactions, they were likely to be on the wrong blockchain. The developers said they would be monitoring the network over the next few days to ensure that the system functioned optimally. Trading at Cryptsy was temporarily suspended, upon request, until the issues had been resolved.

On the 3rd of November at 18:28:49 UTC, user "MicroGuy" said:

> "We were anticipating some network issues, that's one reason we requested that Cryptsy pause trading.
>
> Remember, yesterday the network was highly segmented and now today everyone is on the same chain. This is progress. We are now investigating the issues affecting mining and will be making any necessary fixes as warranted. This coin has evolved well past its humble copy-and-paste beginnings and is now starting a new dawn as a unique and viable currency. Changes of this level and magnitude are complex and bugs are to be expected. Rest assured that you're in capable hands and that these issues will be soon resolved.
>
> Thank you for your understanding and patience."

Users were still having problems mining blocks. Some were very upset of wasting their hashing power mining on the wrong chain. User "MicroGuy" pointed out that the project was "experimental software", so these hiccups were likely to happen. A solution to the unfolding problem was ongoing.

On the 4th of November at 13:53:58 UTC, user "MicroGuy" said:

> "[UPDATE] Mandatory Update 0.7.1.4 (Difficulty fixes)
>
> Download Links: http://gldcoin.com/get-started/
>
> Notes: The difficulty algorithm has been fixed. This is a mandatory update, so be sure to do it before the hard fork at 103000 occurs. The hashrate should correct itself over the next day or so. Sorry for the rather frequent updates of late, we are trying to get the situation resolved as quickly as possible."

Less than twenty four hours later, block number 103,000 was reached:

Block #103,000 (Reward 45 GLD) November 5th 2013 at 11:37:07 AM UTC

Although the difficulty algorithm fix introduced by version 0.7.1.4 took effect at block number 103,000, the developers made people aware that it would take several hours for any adjustments to normalise. Mining pools and exchanges were still closed, but there was an exception. CoinEx was still open during this period.

On the 9th of November at 15:15:09 UTC, user "MicroGuy" said:

> "Please share your thoughts on the dynamics of dual-pair trading.
>
> For example on Cryptsy some coins have trading pairs in both BTC and LTC markets. If a buyer/seller visits the exchange and wants to trade the currency how would he go about getting the best deal. Would it not be more complex and require trading in both markets? If so would this not possibly require the buyer or seller to "hesitate" and look for simpler coins to trade?"

Most people concurred that they would prefer the GLD/LTC trading pair removed. There were some people who did not mind both direct trading pairs because it allows someone with Litecoin to directly buy GoldCoin without buying Bitcoin first.

On the 10th of November at 00:40:47, user "MicroGuy" announced the following:

> "Trading has just resumed on Cryptsy. Enjoy!"

Trading on Cryptsy had ceased for one week during the faults with the difficulty code. One day previously, user "MicroGuy" pointed out why the figures on the website www.coinmarketcap.com had been wrong during that time:

> "Just a head's up that the numbers on Coinmarketcap.com are off since Cryptsy paused trading.
>
> Using the last trade at CoinEX.pw and the MtGox last price we should be in 18th place with a
>
> marketcap of $152,281.00 and a coin price over 1/2 cent each."

On the 13th of November at 18:03:56 UTC, user "AZIZ1977" said:

> "Optional Goldcoin Update Version 0.7.1.5 (Mining optimization) has been released.
>
> http://gldcoin.com/get-started"

On the 15th of November at 00:54:21 UTC, user "Stouse49" notified the community at www.gldtalk.org that he had put the GoldCoin Paper Wallet Generator at http://goldcoinwallet.com. He sought testers from the forum before its release.

On the 15th of November at 15:48:04 UTC, user "MicroGuy" said:

> "It's back and better than ever!!
>
> We're pleased to announce that the Goldcoin (GLD) Android App has just been updated and is now compatible with the new Goldcoin 51% defense system. The latest update is now available for download on the Google Play Store.
>
> Discussion thread >> https://www.gldtalk.org/index.php?topic=555.0
>
> Thanks for all your support! And "may all your bitcoin dreams turn to gold!""

Two days later, two polls went live on the Official GoldCoin Forum. They were submitted by user "Stouse49" on separate threads:

> Poll number one: How did you hear about GoldCoin?
>
> Poll number two: Why did you join the GoldCoin forum (gldtalk.org)

There were several choices available to members of the forum on both polls. It was apparent in the second poll that members were able to chose two reasons why they joined www.gldtalk.org. Both polls would stay open for one month and the corresponding results can be seen in the next chapter of this book.

On the 18th of November at 14:44:55 UTC, user "MicroGuy" said:

> "The giveaway was been halted temporarily due to multiple account abuse. Once we figure out a way to prevent this fraud we'll resume the giveaway. Maybe we will pay a bonus to members who add a social network icon to their profiles.
>
> Thank you for understanding."

However, user "MicroGuy" did send undisclosed amounts of GLD to newbies who posted something creative or interesting.

Throughout the first half of November, the market capitalisation was increasing:

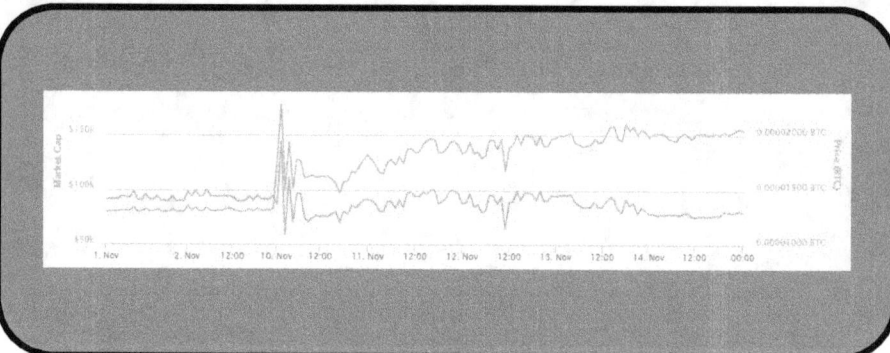

On the 25th of November at 22:06:33 UTC, user "MicroGuy" said:

> "The defense protects the network by preventing hashpower from being added to quickly.
>
> It basically gives more power to the little guy by removing the advantage of someone using an industrial strength mining rig jumping on the network for some quick and easy coins. Mining goldcoin is no longer an exercise in raw hashing power.
>
> Akumaburn wrote about this is detail yesterday:
> https://www.gldtalk.org/index.php?topic=1262.msg6081#msg6081"

On the 24th of November, there was a slight issue with the difficulty calculation. A patch was promised by the developers who were addressing the problems.

On the 26th of November, it was noted that unpredictable mining was still occurring. A low hashrate was being registered by the client software, but it was in fact medium/high. The developers were in the process of making minor adjustments to the way in which the difficulty of mining blocks would be calculated.

On the 27th of November at 08:20:58 UTC, user "MicroGuy" said:

"The Goldcoin development team has just released mandatory software update V 0.7.1.6.

Fixed difficulty code again, added block queuing without client delay (threaded).
Should normalize difficulty in 1-3 days.
Mandatory forking update at block 11700.

Download links: http://gldcoin.com/get-started/

Support forum: https://www.gldtalk.org/index.php?board=22.0

Notes: For those pulling from github you may have to use the following command before your pull will work:
git stash; git fetch origin; git reset –hard origin/master
Thank you for your patience during this time.

The development team is currently on standby in the event you require technical assistance."

On the 27th of November at 15:31:43 UTC, user "MrJohnny5" notified the community that the market capitalisation had surpassed one million US Dollars for the first time. He posted the following www.coinmarketcap.com screenshot:

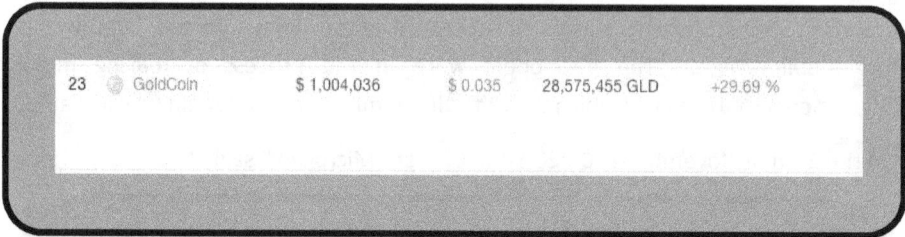

| 23 | GoldCoin | $ 1,004,036 | $ 0.035 | 28,575,455 GLD | +29.69 % |

User "MicroGuy" said that the large market capitalisation rise had a lot to do with the value to Bitcoin increasing as well as the Bitcoin Satoshi value per GLD unit of account.

On the 28th of November at 07:54:28 UTC, user "BitcoinEXpress" said:

"The "51% Protection" is very innovative and I am not being maliciously critical when I say it is broken and needs to be fixed. I want GLD to succeed.

~BCX~"

Block #117,000 (Reward 45 GLD) November 29th 2013 at 08:40:10 AM UTC

At block number 117,000, a total of about 28,639,545 GLD had been mined.

On the 29th of November at 13:54:35 UTC, in response to user "BitcoinEXpress", user "kimosan" said:

"I third BCX's comment.

Still support GLD yet this needs to be fixed."

During the last week of November 2013, the Bitcoin Satoshi value of one unit of GLD account increased considerably. In the table immediately below, the relevant values derived from the cryptocurrency exchange called Cryptsy were:

	Price	Low	Open	Close	High	Volume (BTC)
23rd Nov	1,174	880	1,148	1,200	1,247	6.43746
24th Nov	1,638	1,179	1,195	2,081	2,750	15.9781
25th Nov	2,501	1,751	2,002	3,000	3,000	8.78372
26th Nov	3,251	2,344	3,000	3,502	3,794	14.0766
27th Nov	3,745	2,349	3,489	4,001	4,045	3.36512
28th Nov	3,369.5	2,703	2,703	4,036	4,100	15.6183
29th Nov	5,018	3,800	4,036	6,000	6,000	39.7706
30th Nov	8,994	5,292	6,000	11,988	14,995	75.1476

source: www.cryptocoincharts.info

Other events which occurred in the month of November were:

- On the 6th of November, user "MicroGuy" advertised a position for an experienced forum moderator whose job it would be to welcome newbies who had registered on www.gldtalk.org. They would also be responsible for sending 100 GLD to each new forum member there. However, this promotion was suspended indefinitely twelve days later.

- On the 30th of November, GoldCoin was added to the site http://coinwik.org/GoldCoin. Many useful links and resources can still be accessed from there. However, it is only updated occasionally.

Daily Gold

Friday, Dec 20, 2013

Goldcoin A Worldwide Digit

Another Chance For Investors Who Missed the Early Days of Bitcoin. Price is still low, invest in the future currency Goldcoin. Go to gldcoin.com download your FREE wallet goto cryptsy.com buy gld (Gold) and be prepared to start making some money join us in discussion and find out why Goldcoin is the future of all crypto-currencys @ gldtalk.org and join in on the fun. we have a really great team, that is willing to help get you started on this opportunity of a lifetime. dont wait another minute go to gldcoin.com today!! May All Your Bitcoin Dreams, Turn To GOLD!!

ALL TIME HIGH MARKET CAPITALISATION
OF GOLDCOIN ATTAINED
DECEMBER 2013

I.   An all time high market capitalisation of about $4,854,312 reached.

II.   Version 0.7.1.7 of the wallet client released.

III.   Work began on the first GoldCoin Promotional Video.

IV.   A Bitcoin Satoshi all time high recorded (one GLD) at 15,000.

V.   Results published of the two polls initiated in November 2013.

During the last week of November, the market capitalisation of the coin surged. On the first day of December, the all time high was reached at about $4,854,312. According to www.cryptocoincharts.info, the Bitcoin Satoshi value of one unit of GLD account reached a high of 13,995 on Cryptsy on that same day.

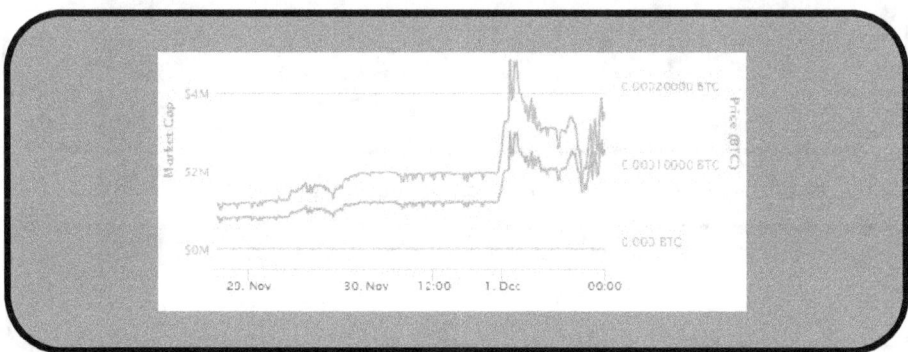

On the 2nd of December at 00:21:23 UTC, user "MicroGuy" posted a status update concerning a future wallet client:

> "A slight problem was discovered in the code that is causing some network difficulties.
>
> There was a blocktime vector error in the code that have been isolated and fixed. The developers are now in the process of preparing this maintenance patch for release. It will be necessary for Cryptsy to pause trading in order to update their wallets."

A few hours later, the code had been patched and verified. The developers made the community aware of an imminent wallet client release. Version 0.7.1.7 was released slightly after the above post.

On the 6th of December at 20:41:43 UTC, user "akumaburn" notified the gldtalk.org community of another future wallet release. He was quoted as saying:

> "Hey everyone,
>
> Our next minor client release (7.2.0) will likely perfect the 51% defense system. I've been working on a way that addresses all varieties of the 51% attack and have found a viable solution.
>
> We're still going over the theoretical parts of the additions to the system but we should have this done by the 18th of December.
>
> Once that happens we will move into phase 2 which is marketing.
>
> I expect a sharp rise in value to occur when this happens.
>
> We're almost there, just a little longer."

Three days later at 07:33:06 UTC, user "bustingbuster" posted the following:

| 19 | GoldCoin | $ 2,817,379 | $ 0.098 | 28,828,805 GLD | +120.02 % |
| 20 | BBQCoin | $ 2,784,329 | $ 0.098 | 28,291,369 BQC | +59.47 % |

On the 9th of December at 15:34:49 UTC, user "MicroGuy" posted the following:

> "We're all very fortunate in that community member crome514 has agreed to begin work on the very first professionally produced Goldcoin video. Look for a project rough draft to be released this week.
>
> To make a contribution towards production costs please use one of the following addresses:
>
> GLD = EBRsmtaie7ebnCzVgkiYdSMpFh4FkCYBnp
> BTC= 13J85a4jF3kHYTC3E5TkNXoTbku8ovuDsQ
>
>
>
> Please also feel free to offer your ideas and suggestions in the thread below."

User "crome514" said he was keen put together a promotional video for GoldCoin. He referred to videos which he put together for other unrelated projects. A promotional video similar to the one created for Bitcoin was sought after by user "MicroGuy". The community would have to wait until January 2014 for the completed video.

Four days later, user "Stouse49" posted instructions on how to use the GoldCoin Paper Wallet at http://goldcoinwallet.com. If unaware beforehand, users of GoldCoin could confidently and securely store their GLD on an offline medium.

On the 17th of December, the results of the two polls were known:

> Poll number one: How did you hear about GoldCoin? (closed at 07:46:18 UTC)
>
> A friend 9 (17.6%); Other 9 (17.6%); The GoldCoin Report (with your Host MicroGuy) on youtube 6 (11.8%). Total Members voted: 47
>
> Poll number two: Why did you join the GoldCoin forum (gldtalk.org)
> (closed at 07:58:07 UTC)
>
> I want to be part of a team that surpasses Litecoin and Bitcoin 20 (46.5%); Other 6 (14%); The GoldCoin Report 6 (14%) Total Members voted: 32

On the 17th of December at 23:58:39 UTC, user "akumaburn" posted:

> "Sorry guys will have to delay it a bit longer.. This Christmas season has been more eventful than most."

He was referring to the next release of the wallet client. As mentioned previously, he said he had begun to perfect the code ready for a release (version 0.7.2.0).

On the 23rd of December at 17:38:18 UTC, use "crome514" said:

> "I just wanted to keep everyone abreast of the situation. The promo video is coming along fairly well. It's taken a little longer to complete than expected (It's Christmas season, and work has been insane for me the last few weeks) but with everything winding down and a holiday week on the horizon, I expect to finish the rough draft within the next few days. I'm aiming for Christmas day.
>
> I didn't forget about it, and thank you all for the donations. It certainly helped with the royalties for some of the assets in the video.
>
> - D"

During the middle of December, the Bitcoin Satoshi values of one unit of GLD account on Cryptsy were decreasing. A Bitcoin Satoshi all time high of 15,000 on this exchange was recorded on the 12th of December:

	Price	Low	Open	Close	High	Volume (BTC)
12th Dec	12,762.5	10,500	12,526	12,999	15,000	41.4089
15th Dec	11,967	10,004	11,988	11,946	12,250	9.43737
18th Dec	9,204.5	7,010	9,910	8,499	10,049	14.4577
21st Dec	7,773	6,936	8,146	7,400	8,246	12.2496
24th Dec	6,310	5,507	6,020	6,600	7,459	5.65771

source: www.cryptocoincharts.info

On the 27th of December at 00:55:29 UTC, user "akumaburn" had further news concerning the upcoming wallet client release:

> "Edit: Scratch that... may take a bit longer.
> I'm starting from a brand new self-written code base...
> so this may take a while..
> Have started on the initial framework, will update you further post holidays."

On the 30th of December at 05:54:37 UTC, user "tadspoles" said:

> "I asked a while back if anyone could make a reddit tip bot. Are there any programmers that can do this? I believe this REALLY helped DogeCoin with exposure."

The idea of a tipbot on Reddit did not gain much interest. This was understandable considering that community presence there, in terms of numbers, was insignificant. As mentioned immediately above in the quote, Dogecoin had an immense Reddit community early on after its launch on the 8th of December 2013.

Other events which occurred in the month of December were:

- On the 9th of December, user "Vincent" thought it necessary to introduce GoldCoin to Chinese cryptocurrency exchanges.

- On the 11th of December, a pre-beta launch of a GLD online marketplace https://gldmarket.com (initially supported GLD, LTC and USD) went live. At this stage, only users willing to test for bugs/faults were allowed to register.

- On the 20th of December, www.gldtalk.org user "Zeuxis" proposed a GoldCoin Foundation

- User "Zeuxis" asked the game website www.rapidballs.eu whether they would add GLD on the 22nd of December. An official member of GLD Development Team had to request the addition.

GOLDCOIN PROMOTIONAL VIDEO PUBLISHED

JANUARY 2014

I.   Who is responsible for the official website at www.gldcoin.com?

II. A promotional video titled "What is GoldCoin?" uploaded to YouTube.

III. "GoldCoin Accepted Here" graphics published.

IV. Facebook Group at https://www.facebook.com/groups/goldcointalk/

V.   Two additional developers sought after.

At the beginning of 2014, the market capitalisation of GoldCoin was at about $1.65 million according to www.coinmarketcap.com.

Also on the first day of the year, user "4DaysMining" announced http://localgoldcoin.com had gone live. His/her post at 14:50:16 UTC included:

"What we are: A P2P marketplace that allows trading of GoldCoin, goods and services. Think a cross of LocalBitcoins and Craigslist.

What we offer: Free Classified Ad postings of GoldCoins, goods and services. Low cost escrow service (3% of transaction). Web Link Repository of mining pools, exchanges and websites currently accepting GoldCoins as form of payment.

What are our plans: To become your #1 spot for selling and buying goods and services with GoldCoin."

On the 4th of January, user "dille71" wanted to know who was responsible for the website www.gldcoin.com. He thought the website required further improvements in terms of available GoldCoin services on the homepage. On the same day at 21:44:37 UTC, user "MicroGuy" responded by saying:

> "The official website is a community owned and operated website.
> I agree that it should be regularly updated and welcome your thoughts, ideas, and suggestions on how it can be improved."

On the 6th of January, the highly anticipated GoldCoin Promotional Video had been completed and subsequently uploaded to YouTube. User "crome514" did not feel his narration was suitable, so encouraged others to improve upon it. He was willing to receive feedback positive or otherwise. On the following day, he proposed a campaign to promote it to a wider audience (see page 102 for video graphics).

On the 8th of January at 20:42:11 UTC, user "psionin" said:

> "Can someone add a Work Items subcategory under Project Development?
> Rather than general discussion and potentially long term ideas, it would include specific things that can be done in a reasonable amount of time.
>
> Threads can be discussed, volunteered for, and also approved/rejected.
> Ex: I wanted to ask for a logo to be created that would fit in with these:"

As a result of the above, user "MicroGuy" created a child board titled "ChalkBoard" for current work related items at https://www.gldtalk.org/index.php?board=46.0.

As requested by user "psionin", work began to design and publish "GoldCoin Accepted Here" graphic images. On the gldtalk.org thread titled "Logo Request: GoldCoin Accepted Here", six designs were submitted by three different people:

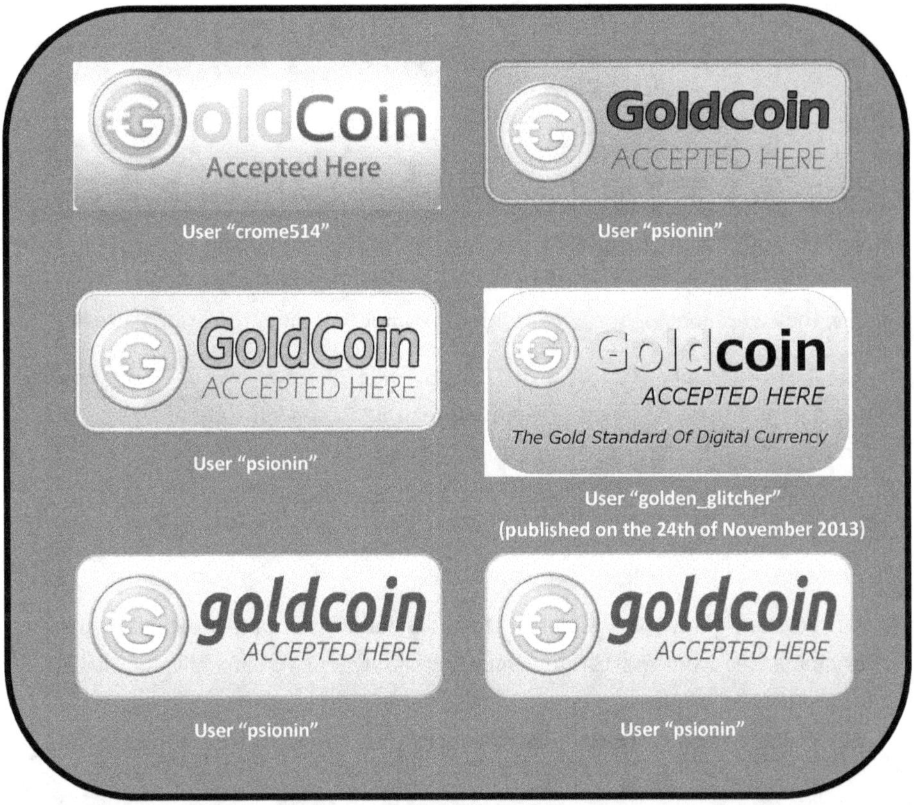

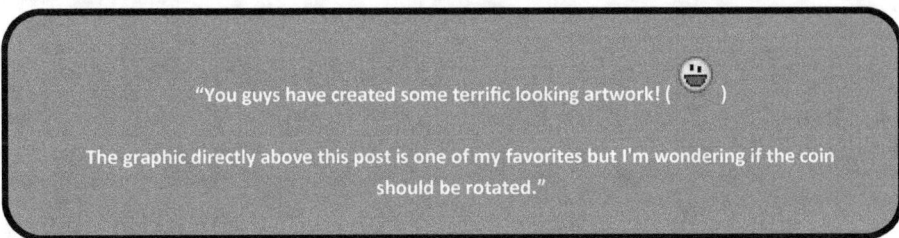

On the 18th of January at 15:17:18, user "MicroGuy" gave his opinion on the above:

"You guys have created some terrific looking artwork! (😃)

The graphic directly above this post is one of my favorites but I'm wondering if the coin should be rotated."

He was referring to the bottom left "GoldCoin Accepted Here" graphic.

On the 16th of January, the community were reminded that a complete rewrite of the wallet client from scratch (multi-threaded code base) was underway. Other unique features were planned, but were kept secret at the time. A few days beforehand, user "akumaburn" said the following:

> Client's on the way.. I hesitate to say when as it is a large undertaking.. but its going well so far."

User "MicroGuy" went onto say that more developers, to work in a supporting role under the guidance and direction of the existing development team, were needed. Ideally, they were looking for two additional competent and professional people.

On the 21st of January at 15:03:20 UTC, user "dille71" on www.gldtalk.org notified the community that the value of GoldCoin had just risen substantially. He posted the following graphic (cropped screenshot) from www.coinmarketcap.com:

| 25 | GoldCoin | $ 1,225,806 | $ 0.042 | 29,413,760 GLD | $ 11,464 | +42.90 % |

As can be seen below, the Bitcoin Satoshi values of one unit of GLD account on Crypsy increased from the 19th of January (the lowest BTC Satoshi value of GLD in January 2014).

	Price	Low	Open	Close	High	Volume (BTC)
19th Jan	2,975	2,856	2,875	3,075	3,201	1.83499
20th Jan	3,326.5	3,028	3,103	3,550	4,000	5.34536
21st Jan	4,647	3,963	3,963	5,331	5,950	8.05884
22nd Jan	4,970.5	4,050	5,352	4,589	5,720	5.00304
23rd Jan	3,719.5	3,500	3,853	3,586	3,906	0.498396

source: www.cryptocoincharts.info

On the 27th of January at 13:38:19 UTC, an experienced moderator was sought after. He/she would manage the official Reddit community of the coin:

> "This individual will be responsible for adding regular content, graphical improvements, and day-to-day moderation. A reddit GLD donation address will be published on the page and the moderator will be entitled to all contributions to the page."

On the last day of the month, the GoldCoin "Board of Trustees" consisted of the following four members:

> Amir Eslampanah, Lead Developer, Canada
> Eric Stouse, Mobile Systems, USA
> Greg Matthews, Administrator, USA
> Aziz Ajadi, Market Analyst, The Netherlands

They wanted to know which organisational model would serve the best interest of GLD. Positions to fill came under "Development", "Marketing" and "Operations".

Other events which occurred in the month of January were:

- A promotional video was uploaded to YouTube titled "What is GoldCoin?" On the 17th of January, user "MicroGuy" sent 10 GLD to people who "Liked" the video on YouTube.

- User "MicroGuy" created the Facebook Group https://www.facebook.com/groups/goldcointalk/ on the 10th of January. This is a private group for discussion of GoldCoin news, updates and other relevant topics.

- Also on the 10th of January, GoldCoin was ranked number 24th on the site www.coinmarketcap.com. By filtering out non-mineable cryptocurrencies, it was ranked at 21st position.

- On the 29th of January, user "MicroGuy" began Season Two (Episode One) of the "GoldCoin Report" after his mid-winter break.

A NEW ALTERNATIVE GOLDCOIN
LOGO DESIGN UNVEILED
FEBRUARY 2014

I.   Effort made to sustain discussion on the official GLD Bitcointalk thread.

II.   A possible GoldCoin symbol (₲, Ǥ, ǥ) proposed by user "psionin".

III.   A national political party pledged support to promote the coin.

IV.   A GoldCoin Foundation website created at http://goldcoinfoundation.org.

V.   Graphics published of an alternative incorporated GoldCoin logo design.

During January, sixteen posts were submitted on the official GLD Bitcointalk thread. It would be a similar number this month. User "MicroGuy" emphasised how important it was to sustain discussion on Bitcointalk as much as possible so as to attract new members to the community. On the 1st of February at 18:20:07 UTC, user "MicroGuy" notified the www.gldtalk.org community of the following:

> "Please vote for Goldcoin (GLD) in this poll:
> https://bitcointalk.org/index.php?topic=443423.0
>
> Going out into the World and showing our support for GoldCoin makes a World of difference in our quest for greatness."

It was a Bitcointalk poll to vote for GLD to be added to www.rapidBalls.eu.

On the 2nd of February, user "MicroGuy" pointed out further Bitcointalk discussion threads on which he encouraged community participation:

"Each day I see new and excited people on Bitcointalk.org eager to become involved in cryptocurrencies.

By remaining active on BCT we can assist these people in finding Goldcoin. In addition many investors and traders base their buying decisions directly on the activity level of the coin's community on BCT.

The top three boards to stay active on:

Main Bitcoin Discussion = https://bitcointalk.org/index.php?board=1.0
Beginners & Help = https://bitcointalk.org/index.php?board=39.0
Alternate Cryprocurrencies = https://bitcointalk.org/index.php?board=67.0

The threads listed above are only a small fraction of the discussions that could benefit from our comments and participation. Feel free to add links to the discussions that you find. And as always, your suggestions and ideas are welcome and appreciated."

On the following day at 17:08:23 UTC, user "psionin" suggested a GLD symbol:

"I've come across these and wanted to share.

Ǥ G g

The one that's probably closer to what we're looking for is the Kadiweu variation of the partially voiced palatal spirant in the Latin Skolt Sami alphabet. (Below, right)

Unfortunately, the international keyboard doesn't appear to include this symbol. Anyone know how to get a symbol added to the international keyboard? Is it something that Microsoft does or is there another organization?"

On the 10th of February, user "MicroGuy" announced on www.gldtalk.org that a national political party had contacted the GoldCoin community. They were willing to support and integrate GoldCoin. User "MicroGuy" viewed this event as very exciting, and an opportunity to further integrate the coin into the mainstream. The initiative was being lead by Darcy Neal Donnelly who posted:

"WOW! Can you imagine a national government endorsing, supporting and accepting cryptic currencies such as GoldCoin as voluntary contributions towards supporting government operations. How would a government operate without its authority to extort taxes from its citizens? Would the citizenship voluntary offer "tips" to support its government? Would the people and associations prefer to be TAXED or to offer TIPS to its government? How would a government living on tips survive? If free enterprises and people can live on "tips", government ought to be able. What's your opinion?"

On the 19th of February at 03:00:04 UTC on www.gldtalk.org, user "MicroGuy" announced the following:

"I've started a website today for the Goldcoin Foundation.
Website: http://goldcoinfoundation.org

If you're interested in helping to setup the foundation please let me know by PM.

Requirements:

1. - Must have Skype account for communications.
2. - Must have Facebook account with completed profile.
3. - Must have GLDTalk.org account.
4. - Must have phone number that be can shared with group.

At first we're going to limit the size of the foundation to eight members. We already have several that have expressed interest on Facebook but there are several spots left.

[Note: This is a "Team Page" I just started on the official website:
http://gldcoin.com/our-team/]"

Unfortunately, progress with a GoldCoin Foundation did not catch on.

Four days later, user "hiburak" announced that voting to get GoldCoin on the exchange called MintPal had begun. However, this exchange never added the coin to its platform. MintPal no longer exists:

"I just got GLD added to the public voting page of MintPal:

https://www.mintpal.com/voting

MintPal is a new crypto-currency exchange site. It just got launched this month and it appears that they have a very responsive support team.

Periodically, they will select the top coin from the list and add it to their website. Unregistered users can vote for 3 times per hour and registered users can vote for 6 times per hour.

Also, each 0.00005000 BTC sent to 1HN2bw9y7mBRoWdi3ceGLfMfV71fYSJWon will count for 1 vote for GoldCoin."

On the 24th of February, a brand new GoldCoin logo design was unveiled (see graphic immediately below and on page number 108). This design is still used to represent the coin, but the logo published by user "Sting17" on the 19th of July 2013 is predominantly used on official websites and elsewhere.

On the 24th of February, user "MicroGuy" published a sneak preview of the new GoldCoin Foundation Homepage:

Special thanks was given to Darcy Neal Donnelly for his contribution towards the new GoldCoin Slogan (above image "Peace, Liberty, and Goldcoin for the People.").

Other events which occurred in the month of February were:

- Voting to get GoldCoin on MintPal was in progress during the month.

- On the 5th of February at 02:10:27 UTC, user "MicroGuy" revitalised his own contact website at http://www.microguy.com/. He had had this domain for a while and it had been sitting idle for years.

- On the 13th of February, the site www.coinmarketcap.com for the first time, had 100 cryptocurrencies listed on its site.

- On the 25th of February, the market capitalisation of GoldCoin increased 50% as MtGox (an infamous Bitcoin trading exchange) closed up shop.

The *Gold Standard*
of Digital Currency

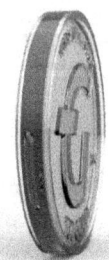

GOLDCOIN BEGAN TO TRADE ON BITTREX

MARCH 2014

I.   A song called "Everybody's Doing The GoldCoin Rap" was published.

II.   Effort made to send someone to the Crypto Convention in New York City.

III.   An updated version of the GoldCoin Android App on the Google Play Store.

IV.   Bittrex began to actively trade GoldCoin on their exchange platform.

V.   A Trello Dashboard was created by user "Viscis".

On the 1st of March at 20:18:47 UTC, user "MicroGuy" advertised a short rap song specifically for GoldCoin titled "Everybody's Doing The GoldCoin Rap". User "tadspoles" described it as "pretty darn good". It was uploaded here:

https://soundcloud.com/greg-matthews-11/everybodys-doing-the-goldcoin

On the following day, user "psionin" published a promotional poster for GoldCoin (see the adjacent page).

On the 5th of March, user "IrishTR" wondered whether the GoldCoin community was going to send a representative to the Cryptocurrency Convention in New York City at the Scholastic Auditorium. User "MicroGuy" said he would, but could not due to personal circumstances. He encouraged others to speak at the event.

Following on from the initial discussion about the upcoming Cryptocurrency Convention in New York City at the Scholastic Auditorium, user "IrishTR" set up a fundraiser at www.indiegogo.com:

"Raising funds to send our representative for GoldCoin to speak on the communities behalf and spread the word of GoldCoin at the CryptoCurrency Con in New York.

Short Summary

We are the GoldCoin CryptoCurrency Community a foundation backed and funded by the community for the community to achieve common goals. This campaign will actually accomplish several goals. First it will help fund our guest speaker/representative to attend the Cryptocurrency Convention in New York on April 9th 2014 http://www.cryptocurrencyconvention.com , and thus add exposure to our community and the GoldCoin standard as well as show the power and potential of GoldCoin. Secondly it will also be proof as to how strong a community, as the GoldCoin Foundation, we are in that we can unite and achieve a common goal for a greater good that all benefit and prosper from.

We are trying to get a minimum of $1000.00 USD in funds for our speaker to represent GoldCoin at the CryptoCurrency Convention to expand the awareness and knowledge of what our coin and community can do. This money raised will go towards airfare and lodging and all costs incurred for this trip."

Unfortunately, on the 15th of March, $360 (fell short of $1,000) had been raised by seven backers in eight days. Over the next few days, efforts were made to look for a well-spoken and knowledgeable GoldCoin individual, but to no avail.

On the 22nd of March, the Bitcoin Satoshi values of one unit of GLD account on Cryptsy were as follows:

	Price	Low	Open	Close	High	Volume (BTC)
20th March	1,772.5	1,630	1,637	1,908	2,001	3.80113
21st March	2,048.5	1,842	1,908	2,189	2,846	4.84461
22nd March	1,986	1,637	2,172	1,800	2,287	2.59894

source: www.cryptocoincharts.info

On the 23rd of March, the Bittrex cryptocurrency exchange initiated trading of the coin. Bittrex began operations on the 13th of February 2014 in beta testing mode and is based in Seattle, Washington in the United States of America. Bittrex fully launched on the 28th of February 2014 with twelve cryptocurrencies and twenty one trading pairs. At the time of publication of this book, GoldCoin no longer trades on this platform.

On the 25th of March, www.gldtalk.org user "Viscis" created a project development board on Trello. It was created to keep track of current goals, delegation, and task progression. It was accessible at this domain:

https://trello.com/b/s0hEvXYH/current-goals

Other events which occurred in the month of March were:

- On the 17th of March, the community were made aware that CoinEx had been hacked. Some people successfully withdrew their GLD holdings from there. It ceased trading shortly after the hacking occurred

- On the 22nd of March, user "MicroGuy" asked for someone to help update and maintain the website at http://www.reddit.com/r/goldcoin.

GOLDCOIN ADDED TO BRAVENEWCOIN

APRIL 2014

I.   Price of GoldCoin increased by about 50% during the first week.

II.   GoldCoin added to the C-Cex cryptocurrency exchange voting list.

III.   An updated wallet client to protect against the HeartBleed Bug was released.

IV.   A chatbox added to the official GoldCoin Forum at www.gldtalk.org

V.   GoldCoin added to the website www.bravenewcoin.com.

On the second day of the month, www.gldtalk.org user "dchoquette" was curious to know if the latest increase in the value of GoldCoin and the decrease in Bitcoin value signalled that GoldCoin was gaining ground on Bitcoin. On this day at 22:02:11 UTC, user "MicroGuy" responded by saying:

> "There are many factors in play. I think as consumers become more and more aware of alternative currencies, they will begin asking questions like, "if Bitcoin and Goldcoin are basically technological equals (it could be argued GLD is superior but that's another discussion), why is bitcoin $500 and the coin with a better name only a penny?""

As can be seen on the next page, the value of one unit of GLD account was 1,900 Bitcoin Satoshi on the opening day of April according to www.cryptocoincharts.info.

During the first few days of the month, the value of one GLD unit of account surged by approximately 50%. The table below displays the values derived from Cryptsy. As is evident, there was a peak in daily trading volume on this exchange on the 4th of April. This was the highest volume since the 13th of December 2013. On the 5th of April, the market capitalisation was about $480,000.

	Price	Low	Open	Close	High	Volume (BTC)
1st April	1,919.5	1,900	1,900	1,939	2,000	1.40743
2nd April	2,145.5	1,931	1,939	2,352	2,755	3.80128
3rd April	2,649.5	2,208	2,526	2,773	3,000	7.61324
4th April	3,150	2,646	2,750	3,550	3,579	30.4392
5th April	3,175	2,799	3,550	2,800	3,570	5.37485

source: www.cryptocoincharts.info

On the 5th of April at 15:59:53 UTC, www.gldtalk.org user "IrishTR" said:

"Hey all sorry for the delay. I recently took a dive down a flight of stairs and broke my arm like a dummy...

Anyways I finally was able to pickup some nice polos and t-shirts and got them dropped off at the embroiderers the polos will be embroidered with our main logo/slogan and the t-shirts will be silk screened with the goldcoin accepted here logo. Once they are completed this week I'll work on getting then mailed out to the folks who contributed. Then post some photos here if anyone else wants to order any.

Again I'll post final photos once done!"

Four days later, photos were published of the GoldCoin embroidered polo shirts made from polyester. One of these is on page 118. User "IrishTR" said they were still in progress. He wanted to know how many people were interested in purchasing so he could go ahead with putting in an order from his supplier.

On the 8th of April at 03:45:07 UTC, gldtalk user "dchoquette" created a thread in order to request a regular report from the community. He had noticed that other cryptocurrencies were releasing regular weekly, biweekly or monthly articles, newsletters or videos. He thought it would make GoldCoin more professional and authenic. User "MicroGuy" was still creating videos for the Goldcoin Report at this time. On the same day at 11:12:37 UTC, user "MicroGuy" replied:

> "This would be a great project for someone that keeps up with the daily news and events within the community. Maybe it could be a regular "week in review" type newsletter or report.
> Off the top of my head from last week:
>
> 1. Sizzflair was appointed moderator of the Goldcoin Reddit http://www.reddit.com/r/goldcoin and also created a new mining subreddit: http://www.reddit.com/r/GoldCoinMining
>
> 2. IrishTR announced that the Goldcoin polo shirts would be completed this week. https://www.gldtalk.org/index.php?topic=2444.0
>
> 3. The price of Goldcoin is up around 50% on the week. http://coinmarketcap.com/mineable.html
>
> 4. We announced in the Facebook group that the new client will be capable of supporting other cryptocurrencies like Bitcoin and Litecoin: https://www.facebook.com/groups/goldcointalk/
>
> 5. There was an article about how the IRS ruling is favorable to the long-term outlook of Goldcoin:http://altcoinpress.com/2014/03/irs-ruling-supports-digital-gold-argument/"

On the 9th of April at 15:09:31 UTC, www.gldtalk.org user "c-cex" said:

> "Added by user requests: https://c-cex.com/?id=vote Welcome to voting!"

Members of community could now support the coin's addition. GoldCoin would finally begin trading there on the 5th of September 2015. At the time of publication of this book, most daily trading volume of GLD against BTC and USD occurs there.

Also on the 10th of April at 01:41:20 UTC, user "MicroGuy" posted the following update on both the official gldtalk.org forum and Bitcointalk forum thread:

"April 9, 2014: The Windows 0.7.1.7 client has been updated to fix the OpenSSL Heartbleed bug. It is recommended that all Windows users download and install this security update.

http://gldcoin.com/get-started/"

On the 17th of April at 00:13:15 UTC, www.gldtalk.org user "bravenewcoin" made the GoldCoin community aware of the following:

"Hello Crypto World

We are proud to announce http://bravenewcoin.com/ and that Goldcoin has been listed.

"In this Brave New World of crypto-currency, a solid and transparent Price-index and Global Spot price is essential""

They are described as "A Data and Research company focused on the Blockchain and Digital Equities industry". A vast array of historical charts, coin specifications and news articles can be found there. Below is the historical chart for GoldCoin:

Initial USD per GLD value recorded on www.bravenewcoin.com was $0.01706466

On the 15th of April, user "MicroGuy" announced the following:

> "After nearly a solid year of requests, the Goldcoin Forum finally gets chat! Tomorrow the API will be upgraded to handle 60 simultaneous users."

This was an valuable addition to the GoldCoin Forum. Members could now chat to each other in real time, therefore have discussions about coin related material.

On the 28th of April, user "MicroGuy" notified the community of the "May 2014 Community Member of the Month" award. Nominations were open until the end of the month. The winner would win a free ASIC Gridseed miner along with 5000 GLD.

On the last day of the month, user "MicroGuy" welcomed someone to create a new GoldCoin Faucet (a means by which people can be donated a small amount of GLD from a source of prior donated coins).

Other events which occurred in the month of April were:

- On the 16th of April, user "Viscis" wanted GoldCoin on the website at http://www.coingecko.com/. It is a site on which hundreds of cryptocurrencies are ranked according to several indicators such as social media presence and developer activity.

- On the 19th of April, user "akumaburn" (Amir Eslampanah) was appointed administrator of https://www.facebook.com/groups/goldcointalk/.

ONE YEAR ANNIVERSARY OF GOLDCOIN

MAY 2014

I.   A new wallet client almost ready for testing.

II.   GoldCoin Polo Shirts manufactured and ready for sale.

III.   GoldCoin included in a poll titled "Altcoin Poll - 2014/15".

IV.   A total number of 169,189 blocks during the first year.

V.   Last block of the first year timestamped on the 15th of May at 00:42:24 UTC.

On the first day of the month, user "MicroGuy" received confirmation from the developers that a new client was almost ready for testing. In addition to this news, he posted the following on the same day at 21:52:43 UTC in response to user "dreamwatcher":

> "Thank you for your work in maintaining the block explorer. It's an invaluable resource for the entire community."

To be specific, it was in reference to the official GoldCoin block explorer gld.cryptocoinexplorer.com (formally at the URL gold.cryptocoinexplorer.com. It was important to safeguard a reliable block explorer for use by the community and for technical reasons.

On the 2nd of May at 17:05:15 UTC, user "IrishTR" announced the following:

> "Shirts are done and picking up today will get final photo and drop them off at the post office tomorrow! Finally! Thank you everyone for waiting patiently. Future orders should only take a week tops since all the design and layout troubles are over with!"

On the 4th of May at 01:47:25 UTC, a Bitcointalk poll was submitted titled "Altcoin Poll - 2014/15" by user "davidwolf". He was quoted as saying:

> "Please pick 3 of the most promising alternate coins
>
> Please Explain your choice."

A total of 509 votes were submitted. The top ten cryptocurrencies were:

> Whitecoin: 133 Blackcoin: 104 Mintcoin: 93 Darkcoin: 79 Dogecoin: 77
> Bitcoin: 67 (not altcoin) Vertcoin: 65 Litecoin: 62 Quark: 48 Myriadcoin: 40
> Nxt: 36 Goldcoin came 16th in the poll with 19 votes

On the last https://www.gldtalk.org thread before the coin's one year anniversary, user "sizzflair" at 18:26:46 UTC on the 14th of May described the forum as pretty dead. Reference was made to hardly any updates from the developers and no news about an upcoming wallet client. The term "Pump and Dump" was also used. In response to these comments, user "MicroGuy" at 19:39:53 UTC said:

> "The existing client is performing great and the new client will be ready for testing in early June.
>
> I think the biggest thing we're lacking right now is general community involvement and participation."

User "sizzfliar" continued to say GoldCoin lacked community involvement and exchange presence in comparison to other altcoins. He also said GoldCoin was not attracting sufficient attention and investment interest. User "MicroGuy" said:

"Thank you for your comments.

I see at the moment we're back at #43:
http://coinmarketcap.com/views/filter-non-mineable-and-premined/

This currency is over a year old now and development is ongoing. Not sure how it could ever be misconstrued as just another pump and dump coin. In June, we'll be releasing the new client and it's chock-full of innovations. In terms of "firsts", there will be many in the new client. Akumaburn was originally hoping for a May 21 release, but now it's looking more like sometime in June. I think we're in good shape for a summer surge.

There's a project board here where we're hoping to organize community efforts:
https://www.gldtalk.org/index.php?topic=2423.0"

From the 1st to the 15th of May, there were a total of ten posts submitted on the official Goldcoin Bitcointalk thread. The official forum www.gldtalk.org and the private Facebook group at https://www.facebook.com/groups/goldcointalk/ had become the most popular discussion destinations for the coin.

On the 15th of May, the last block of the first year was timestamped to the blockchain. At block number 169,189, a total of approximately 30,998,050 GLD had been mined.

Block #169,189 (Reward 45 GLD) May 15th 2014 at 12:42:24 AM UTC

Block #169,190 (Reward 45 GLD) May 15th 2014 at 12:55:06 AM UTC

APPENDIX

FIRST GOLDCOIN
PATCH ANNOUNCEMENT
PUBLISHED ON THE
27TH OF JULY 2013

Welcome to the first official GoldCoin Patch Announcement. We have been working tirelessly over the last 6 weeks to bring you these important updates, fixes and features for GoldCoin.

The goals for this particular coin patch were two fold. Firstly to fix some of the coin generation rules created during the first fork and to also fix the issues in the client due to poor coding. We will go into further details on these fixes below.

Coin Patch (Hard Fork)

The main reason for forking GoldCoin was a simple one; the previous fork at 21,000 block mark had removed the limit on coins to be generated and also removed the coin generation rules. This meant two things, the coin would no longer reduce it's coin reward per block from 500 and would also produce 500 coins per block forever.

This creates a number of issues the main one being that with a never ending supply of coins the currency would plummet in price and then die. This was not something we wanted and as such we got to work.

Client Issues

A lot of Litecoin based Crypto Currencies have been suffering from a Syncing and Prefix issue with their respective wallet clients and GoldCoin is no different. This was due to the wallet still using the Litecoin prefix and as such allowing connections from the Litecoin blockchain and in turn throwing the wallet client off course resulting in syncing to the Litecoin blockchain instead. This as well as the alert key not being changed was the cause for the Litecoin Alert messages.

This issue has been fixed along side building the clients from the latest available source, bringing them up to date with Litecoin. We also have many more features in the pipeline for future versions of the client. We are not standing still with the client and will be continually improving and added new features to the wallet.

Changes to Block Rewards

In order to stop inflation due to a never ending supply of coins, we have tried to keep close to the original goal of 100 Million coins but rather stretch this out over 100 years.

This gives the coin an extended lifecycle but also creates a finite amount similar to real world Gold. It also allows the price to continue to rise as adoption and scarcity take hold.

Difficulty Retarget

GoldCoin suffered what some could call an attack back before the 21,000 fork which rendered the network almost unusable. The network was met with a large amount of hashing power resulting in a skyrocketing difficulty. The hashing power was then removed from the network and the difficulty remained high due to the large difficulty retarget period. This is commonly referred to as a Difficulty Attack. It took a number of weeks to mine enough blocks to get the next difficulty retarget point.

To eliminate that we have chosen a much quicker block retarget time of 60 Blocks or roughly 2 hours, making the network less susceptible to these kinds of attacks

GoldCoin Specifications

Pre-Patch Specifications:		Post-Patch Specifications:	
Block Time	2.5 Minutes	Block Time	2 Minutes
Confirmations	6 Confirms (15 Minutes)	Confirmations:	6 Confirms (12 Minutes)
Difficulty Retarget:	504 Blocks (21 Hours)	Difficulty Retarget	60 Blocks (2 Hours)
Block Reward	500	Block Reward	45
Reward Adjustment	0	Reward Adjustment	$50 / (1.1 + 0.49 * n)$
			n = years after fork
Total Coins	∞	Total Coins	123,423,900

GoldCoin Inflation and Supply Information

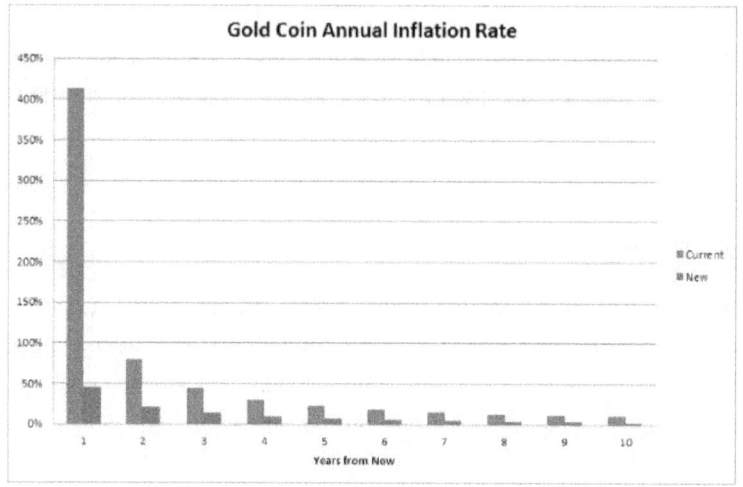

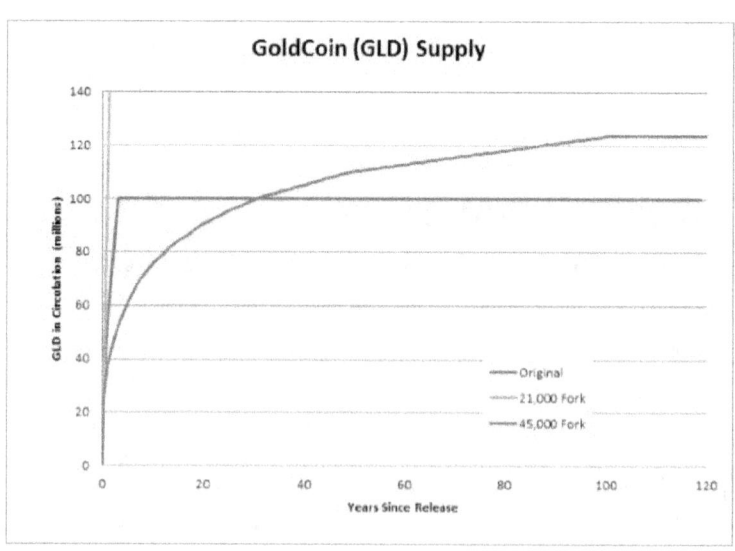

SECOND GOLDCOIN
PATCH ANNOUNCEMENT
PUBLISHED ON THE
11TH OF OCTOBER 2013

GoldCoin Patch Announcement

Welcome to the GoldCoin minor version 7 announcement. We have some fantastic news for you folks today. We have at last solved the greatest problem having to do with crypto-currency, 51% network ownership, whilst keeping standard proof of work! The more people update to this version the less vulnerable to 51% attacks we are. Therefore this is a mandatory update.

What is a 51% attack

In a nut shell, a 51% attacker controls the majority of the network's mining power, and since the network automatically chooses the longest blockchain to be the correct one, this gives the attacker control over transactions. This allows them to repeatedly spend the SAME coins on an exchange over and over again.

A 51% attack is a fundamental problem with all proof of work coins that has existed up until today. Even Bitcoin has not managed to solve this problem. No more will there be multi-mining-pools that simply mine a coin while the difficulty is low and thereafter immediately dump, and no more fear from hash-power attacks because of some server farm!

The impossible made possible

We've been told over and over again, almost to the point of being brainwashed, that there is no solution to the 51% problem with coins that use the proof of work system(Ie: GoldCoin, LiteCoin, BitCoin). That changes today, you may wonder how - but do not fret, everything will be explained below in great detail.

This is a soft forking update. this minor version will be dictating the blockchain regardless of greater lengths in lower versions. However the older versions are forward compatible with this one as long as they remain on the same chain. As of this release we are the only coin to date that can claim resistance to 51% attacks, and post block 100,000 we can claim virtual immunity from them!

"For the longest time the crypto-coin community had to deal with cyber-bullies getting in the way of innovation, -not anymore though with GoldCoin…"

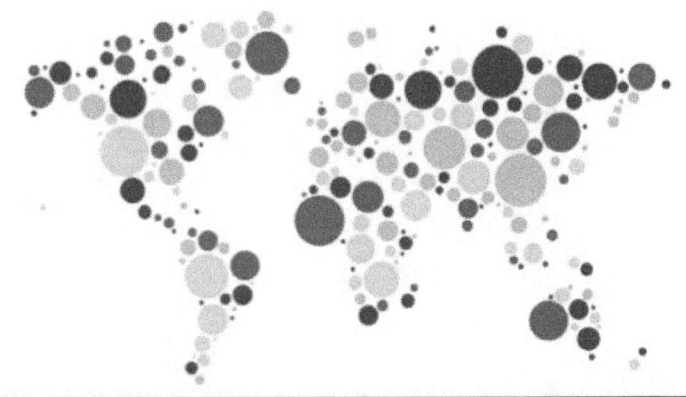

GoldCoin—The Gold Standard of Digital Currency

www.ingramcontent.com/pod-product-compliance
Lightning Source LLC
Chambersburg PA
CBHW070322190526
45169CB00005B/1705